IT'S faux EASY

WITH GARY LORD

NORTH LIGHT BOOKS
CINCINNATI, OHIO
www.artistsnetwork.com

08 07 06 05 04   5 4 3 2 1

Library of Congress Cataloging-in-Publication Data

Lord, Gary
It's Faux Easy with Gary Lord:
Paint 30 Fabulous Finishes for Your Home
p. cm.
ISBN 1-58180-554-3 (pbk. : alk. paper)
1. House painting.
2. Texture painting.
3. Finishes and finishing.

I. Title

TT323.L68 2004
698'.14–dc22

2004049282

Editor: Christina D. Read
Production Coordinator: Kristen Heller
Production Artist: Kathy H. Bergstrom
Designer: Leigh Ann Lentz
Photographer: Tim Grondin

METRIC CONVERSION CHART

TO CONVERT	TO	MULTIPLY BY
Inches	Centimeters	2.54
Centimeters	Inches	0.4
Feet	Centimeters	30.5
Centimeters	Feet	0.03
Yards	Meters	0.9
Meters	Yards	1.1
Sq. Inches	Sq. Centimeters	6.45
Sq. Centimeters	Sq. Inches	0.16
Sq. Feet	Sq. Meters	0.09
Sq. Meters	Sq. Feet	10.8
Sq. Yards	Sq. Meters	0.8
Sq. Meters	Sq. Yards	1.2
Pounds	Kilograms	0.45
Kilograms	Pounds	2.2
Ounces	Grams	28.4
Grams	Ounces	0.04

ABOUT THE AUTHOR

Gary Lord is recognized internationally as an artist, teacher, author and television personality. Gary owns and operates Gary Lord Wall Options and Associates, Inc., which executes all of his commercial and residential decorative finishing contract. Wall Options won first place in two Painting and Decorating Contractors of America national competitions and was named best faux finisher in the nation in 2002 and 20... by Painting and Wallcovering Contractor.

Gary also operates Prismatic Painting Studio, which allows him to teach his extensive finishing skills to others, nationally and internationally.

Gary has appeared on HGTV's *Decorating with Style* and *The Carol Duvall Show*, the show *Paint! Paint! Paint!* and The Discovery Channel's *Christopher Lowell Show.* He writes numerous articles on decorative painting for *Decorative Artist's Workbook, Artist's Magazine, The Faux Finisher, Artistic Stenciler, The Decorative Painter, Profil Faux, Paint Pro, American Painting Contractor* and *Architectural Living,* among others is his third North Light book. He has also written *Great Paint Finishes for a Gorgeous I* and *Marvelous Murals You Can Paint.*

DEDICATION

Life is a very short process in which we need to learn what is really important. I am blessed to be able to make a living at something I love and am happy that others wish to share that with me. But I am really blessed by my wonderful wife Marianne and my great children Ben, Corrie and Jared, for it is their love and support that I enjoy every day.

ACKNOWLEDGEMENTS

In my professional career, I wish to thank the many clients, interior designers, architects, students and each of you who enable me to make a living in one of the most rewarding ways I can think of.

The finished projects in this book reflect many creative and talented artists.

Thank you to my fellow artisans who continue to help me grow in this field and whose work is instrumental in this book: Micah Ballard, Kris Hampton, Dave and Pam Schmidt, Richard Seiler, Jeff Sutherland, Joe Taylor, Dave Texter and Robert Vadnais.

Thank you to Nancy Beal, Cindy Crawford, Ron Hammond, Judy Holland, Pam Monk, June Surber, Henry Vittetoe and Jenny Wynne, whose wonderful sense of interior design and creativity made many of the projects in this book happen.

A Special Thanks to my clients who allowed their beautiful homes to be photographed: Mr. and Mrs. Biedermann, Mr. and Mrs. Brown, Mr. and Mrs. Carlisle, Mr. and Mrs. Chapman, Mr. and Mrs. Gerlinger, Mr. Kalic, Mr. and Mrs. Kurz, Mr. and Mrs. Luggen, Mr. and Mrs. McFarland, Mr. and Mrs. Morris, Mr. and Mrs. Murad, Mr. and Mrs. Pickard, Mr. and Mrs. Raizk, Mr. and Mrs. Ross, Mr. and Mrs. Rust, Mr. and Mrs. Schmitt, Mr. and Mrs. Schweikert, Mr. and Mrs. Siracusa, Mr. and Mrs. Smith, Mr. and Mrs. Summerall, Mr. and Mrs. Veneziano, Mr. and Mrs. Watkoske, Mr. Watson and Ms. Lanter.

Thank you to my wonderful editor, Chris Read, and my photographer, Tim Grondin, for all of their great help.

Thank you to my office manager Shari Evans and my wife Marianne for helping with all the compiling and typing of this book. Without them I would be lost—just ask them.

This book is the result of the collaboration between many people and me. If I have unintentionally left out anyone's name it is my fault alone. I value all my professional relationships and do not take any of them for granted.

TABLE OF CONTENTS

INTRODUCTION

I can think of no more enjoyable way to decorate a home or office than with a hand-painted finish of some kind. Since the beginning of time, society has valued hand-painted finishes as alternatives to other forms of decorating. We have proof from the caves in the Alsace-Lorraine region in France that prehistoric man brought his world into his home with cave paintings. We have had different art styles throughout history: the petroglyphs, Egyptian hieroglyphics, Greco-Roman, Renaissance up to modern styles. We are all using many of the same techniques and effects today that prior generations of artists perfected. For centuries, decorative painting techniques were kept as "trade secrets", with artisans working behind closed doors or shielded by screens so no one could learn their techniques. The information was often passed on only to family members and sometimes information was lost forever. But today many of those "Old World" decorative painting techniques are being shared by authors and schools throughout the world.

In this book, you will learn many valuable painting skills with easy, step-by-step instructions accompanied by detailed photographs showing you the way. Don't be afraid to try anything in this book. The worst thing that can happen is you lose a little of your time and have to repaint an area. Even if you make a mistake, think of it not as a failure but as an opportunity to learn. I can't tell you how many of my own jobs don't go the way I think they will, and I have to change course in midstream. Often, some of my best work comes out of the jobs that were failures.

When you are following a recipe while cooking, you can alter the ingredients a little for a minor taste change or a lot for a dramatic difference. You can do the same with my "paint recipes." Do not be afraid to combine one concept from a chapter with a different technique from another chapter to create your own "secret recipe." You can also change colors to go with your décor. Be creative; it's what makes this process so much fun!

GETTING STARTED

This section will teach you everything you need to know about surfaces, repairs and all the important supplies needed to create any of the beautiful paint techniques featured in this book. By following the directions and tips, you can learn to create simple or more detailed faux wall treatments.

Home of Frank & Lisa Veneziano

ROOM PREPARATION

SURFACE INSPECTION

General surface preparation should start with a close inspection of the areas you are painting. You want to look for any nail pops, stress cracks, dings or dents in the walls, previous patch jobs, loose or bad caulking around moldings, flaking or cracking paint, water marks, smoke damage or dirty surfaces. Make sure you do these inspections while the lighting in the room is good, as it is very easy to miss spots in poor lighting. You could also use a halogen lamp and shine it on your surfaces to help find any problem areas. Usually when I am making my inspection, I use small pieces of blue low-tack adhesive tape to mark any areas in need of repair. I also keep this tape by the areas being repaired until the repair work is complete, since it is often hard to see your spackled spots on white walls. Please note that you should not begin repairing the walls until you have completed the room preparation mentioned later in this section.

PROTECTING THE FLOORS

Cover the floors with drop cloths. Use butyl rubber-backed drop cloths so paint can't soak through them. For hardwood floors or wall-to-wall carpet, I cover the baseboards using a tape dispenser and 6- to 12-inch (15cm to 31cm) craft paper that extends beyond the baseboard to cover the edge of the floor. This saves me a tremendous amount of cleanup in the long run. Even though I put drop cloths over the entire floor, they tend to pull away from the wall, allowing the floor to be exposed to the risk of paint spatters. The paper shield helps protect the floors from paint spatters even if the drop cloth shifts positions.

PROTECTING TRIM & CEILINGS

If I am doing my basecoat, I will not mask out the trim and ceiling areas. I just cut into them with my cut brush. But if I am applying a decorative paint finish, which can be messier, I protect these areas using 2-inch (5cm) blue tape on the trim and, for the ceilings, either 2-inch (5cm) blue tape or 6-inch (15cm) craft paper applied with a tape gun and 1-inch (3cm) blue tape.

PROTECTING FURNITURE

I try to move all small pieces of furniture and pictures out of the room. I throw 9' x 12' (3m x 4m) sheets of plastic over all of the furniture remaining in the room. This may sound like a lot of work, but I have found that if you paint often enough, you will spill paint at some point. For any of my clients who are reading this, I did not spill paint on your job. However, it is better to be safe than sorry. In my career I have spilled paint dozens of times. But because of my good prep work, I have never had to buy a carpet or piece of furniture.

SURFACE REPAIR

Once you prep the room, you can then attend to the areas that need repair. If the walls are extremely dirty or greasy, I wash them first. You can use a product like Soilax or trisodium phosphate to clean the surfaces. Make sure you clean the walls from the floor up to the ceiling. When you clean this way, you avoid streaking the walls with cleaning solution. If you have bare drywall, you need to lightly dust the walls before you prime them to make sure your paint will bond properly to the drywall board.

REPAIRING CRACKING PAINT

Next, I scrape off any loose or cracking paint and then use spackling compound and a putty knife to fill any surface irregularities. Most compounds shrink a little, so leave more on the surface to account for this possible shrinkage. Once the areas are dry, sand them with medium to fine sandpaper till smooth. Sometimes it is easier to feel the texture with your hands than to see it with your eyes. You can spot-prime these areas if there are only a few, but if there are a lot, it is easier just to prime the whole wall.

REPAIRING CAULKING

If the caulking is bad, I remove any loose areas and re-caulk with a good tube of paintable acrylic caulking. It is worth buying the better caulking product because it lasts longer than the inexpensive brands.

SURFACE PREPARATION

There are a variety of needs for different surface preparations. The following outlines are generalizations only, and each area may vary. If you are ever in doubt as to what to do to get an area ready, just make your surface as smooth as possible and clean off any dirt, grease or wax contaminants before painting. At the beginning of each project, I will list the type of paint basecoat and color. All of the projects in this book use 100% water-based materials except for the Rolco Slow Set Gold Size which is an oil-based product and is used for the metallic foil finishes. I switched over to a water-based system about eight to ten years ago, mostly for my health, the safety of my employees and clients, as well as ever-increasing governmental regulations. I can truly say I am happier, and feel I am a better artist with greater products to choose from. So, all prep work in this book is geared for water-based techniques.

OVER OIL-BASED PAINT

First, a tip for you: An easy way to tell if your surface is painted with oil is to take a cotton ball and put denatured or isopropyl alcohol on it. In an obscure area, rub it onto your paint. If the paint is removed or gets soft and gummy, it is a water-based paint. If it stays hard and firm, it is an oil-based paint. If it is an oil-based paint, you should do a light sanding on the surface with a fine to medium sandpaper. Then dust off the surface and apply a water-based paint that will adhere to an oil-based paint surface. There are many of these paints on the market, so just ask your paint dealer. Some of these will be primer coat paints only, like BEN 123, Kilz, Shieldz, and XIM. These all need a water-based finish coat on top if you use a specific color underneath your technique. You can also get water-based paints that are a combination primer and finish coat, such as Aqua Finishing Solutions AquaBond or Porter Paints Advantage 900. Once you have converted your oil paint to a water-based paint system, you can safely do any of the projects in this book.

OVER LATEX

If you are working over any latex-based paint, you need to make sure the paint is clean of any dirt, grease, wax or other contaminant. If the sheen of the existing paint is a semi-gloss or lower sheen, you can usually put latex straight onto latex with no additional prep. If the sheen of the paint is a high gloss, you may need to do a light sanding and tack off the surface prior to painting.

OVER LACQUER

You can paint any latex over lacquer after you have lightly sanded the surface and used a tack cloth to remove any dust residue.

OVER WALLPAPER

Another tip for you: All paint stores and wallpaper manufacturers will tell you to remove all wallpaper and its paste before doing any painting. That is the best way, especially if your walls are a smooth finish. But I do break the rules when it makes sense. For example, clients want to have a dimensional texture applied to their walls and are concerned about the hassle and expense of removing it later. I can save them money by going over their existing wallpaper with a textured finish, if the wallpaper is secure and in sound shape. I make sure the seams and edges of the paper are not loose and are fairly flush. I apply a coat of primer such as an oil-based Shieldz or Bullseye that will act as a stain blocker and primer in one coat. I can apply my dimensional texture right over the existing primed wallpaper. This not only saves the time and expense of removing the paper, but if I want to remove the texture in the future, I can strip off the wallpaper to do so. It is harder removing a painted paper than one that has not been painted, but it is a lot easier getting rid of my texture this way. I have painted textures dozens of times over wallpaper for more than twenty years and have never once had a failure.

You should warn your client of the potential hazards of the wallpaper releasing or product failures. Have them sign a release to protect you in case of any problems. If you started to remove your wallpaper and the paper is ripping, STOP! You can use a wall primer such as Shieldz by Zinsser right over the ripped-up damaged wall surface. Then do one of your heavier dimensional finishes over the walls and you will save yourself countless hours and frustration.

BASIC TECHNIQUES

OVER DAMAGED WALLS

If you are doing a smooth decorative painting finish, you need your walls as smooth as possible. You need to patch any nail pops, dings, dents, cracks, scratches, etc. with drywall mud, then sand the patch smooth to the surface and dust it off. Now use any drywall primer to either spot prime or prime out the whole room with it. If you are doing a dimensional texture, you can go right over most minor flaws. Use common sense as to what may need additional work, the repair needed and the depth of your finished texture.

BASECOATING TECHNIQUES

When basecoating your walls in a water-based paint, use a 2½-inch (64mm) sash brush or Whizz roller to cut in around the edges of the room and around the moldings. If you are working by yourself, you can cut and roll the walls at the same time. If you are working with another person, one can cut in while the other rolls the paint on.

Use a 9-inch (23cm) roller frame with a ½-inch (13mm) nap lambskin roller cover to apply the paint. The lambskin covers are more expensive but they hold a lot of paint, spatter very little and clean up very quickly. Try to roll right into the wet cut lines as closely as you can on the edges. You can even turn the roller sideways at the ceiling and baseboards. This avoids the difference you may notice with brush strokes versus roller marks. Also, there is sometimes a minor color difference between paint that has been brushed on versus rolled on, and this technique will help eliminate that problem. I almost always apply two solid basecoats before doing a decorative finish. You need to make sure the paint has dried thoroughly between coats and before you start your decorative finish.

GLAZE COATING TECHNIQUES

There are many ways to apply your glazes in decorative paint finishes, from using brushes and paint rollers of all sizes, as well as rags and cheesecloth, to spraying and other techniques. If using a paint roller, I normally use a ⅜- or ½-inch (10mm or 13mm) Whizz Premium Gold Stripe roller cover on a 9-inch (23cm) roller frame or 4-inch (10cm) Whizz roller. Each step in the glazing process, from the application to completion, affects the final look. In this book, I will describe many different ways to apply your glazes.

One of the most important things in your decorative painting process is consistency. Make sure that the process is the same throughout. If you are using two or more people to do a finish, make sure each person does the same job throughout to help maintain this consistency. For example, the same person who rolls on the glaze should do it everywhere while the other person takes the glaze off with a rag. Pay close attention to your edges and corners and use a 2-inch (51mm) chip brush to pounce your glaze in these areas and even it out.

FOIL INSTALLATION

Foils have many possibilities, all depending on how you wish to use them. Here are some general guidelines to follow.

First, always basecoat before foiling. You cannot apply foils over an unpainted surface. Foils can go over any flat, satin, semi-gloss oil- or latex-based paint. Over flat latex, you may need two coats of Rolco size for better transfer of the foil and longer working time. Basecoat the surface with satin latex- or oil-based paint in any color, then apply only one coat of size. Try to select a paint color that is close to the dominant foil color. If you want a strong metallic look, use a metallic paint underneath the foil. Basecoats need to be fully dry before applying size.

You must have the SHINY SIDE UP when transferring foil. Crumple and uncrumple the foil. With a firm, even pressure, rub the foil onto the tacky size. Then remove the backing. A small, short-bristled nylon scrub brush works well for giving maximum release. To avoid obvious seams, apply the foil with a torn, ragged edge. Foils do not usually transfer 100% to your surface; you can expect a 70–90% transfer. If you want 100% coverage, you need to size, apply the foil, then resize over the foil and apply foil again.

For more information, instructional packets and videos on foiling are available from Prismatic Painting Studios (see page 142).

TOOLS, MATERIALS AND PRODUCTS

Every Christmas my staff and I exchange small presents. As I write this at my desk, I am looking at a present I received one year, a miniature wooden, hand-painted cat in a wicker basket. You might be thinking "a cat?" like I did when I received this present. But once Jeff presented it to me, I learned that he thought I was like a cat because I am always curious. It's true, I am constantly wondering how to paint something, or what would happen if I put this product with another in a way I never have before. I think this curiosity is important for all artists because it is with curiosity that creativity begins.

In the field of decorative painting, the possibilities of new and different techniques are endless. I tell my students that art is like music in its vastness. For example, a piano has only eighty-eight keys, but no one has ever come close to figuring out everything that can be done with those eighty-eight keys. I look at the endless variety of paint products, all of the different paint brushes, tools and objects that can be used to create effects as my piano keys, though there are a lot more than eighty-eight painting components.

In this book I use a wide variety of these tools to create different effects. I also use different paint products from different manufacturers. You can find information on these in the back of the book. Almost 99% of this book uses water-based products, which offer easy clean up and are environmentally friendly. This book also showcases products and tools from some of my other favorite manufacturers. I hope you will add this information to your repertoire of techniques.

WATER-BASED PAINT SYSTEMS

Water-based paints are a lot more user-friendly than oil-based paints because they are almost odorless and dry quickly (usually within 2 hours), allowing for multiple applications in one day. This is especially true when applying the basecoats for your decorative paint technique.

Water-based paints are easy to clean up with soap and water. They are healthier for you to use than solvent-based products because they do not release harmful toxins into the air and enter into your skin while you are using them. There are many parts of the country that are now restricting the use of solvent-based paints.

It is for all of these reasons that the majority of the paints mentioned in this book are water-based. Also note that many of the techniques illustrated in this book could not have been developed without the incredible water-based products made by creative paint manufacturers.

BASECOATS

Most of the time you should use a low luster or semi-gloss latex or 100% acrylic paint as your basecoat. A good quality paint will make a difference in how long your glazes will stay open. 100% acrylic paints seem to work better as basecoats because they do not have fillers, clay or silica in them which ultimately affect your open time. Sheen of paint will also affect your open time, as discussed in the next section.

One word of caution: Allow your basecoats to dry twenty-four to forty-eight hours before glazing on them. This will allow the longest open time for your glazes, because the basecoat has dried firmer and the glaze will not bite into it as it will on a softer paint film that is still fresh. You can certainly glaze on a dried film of fresh paint but the glaze sinks in more. It is harder to manipulate, and you may create the dreaded "lap line."

SHEEN

You must choose a degree of paint sheen. Paint that has no sheen is labeled as a flat or matte finish. Paint that has a slight sheen is called satin, low-luster or eggshell. Higher sheens are known as semi-gloss and high-gloss. All paints start out as a high-gloss sheen and flattening agents are added to progressively lower the sheen to the desired level. All major paint stores will have a chart to help you determine sheen.

Generally, the higher the paint sheen, the higher the durability and washability of the surface. It is also generally true that the higher the paint sheen, the longer your open time for glazes. Many negative glazing treatments cannot be done on a flat sheen and certainly should not be tried by a novice faux finisher. Once you become more experienced, you can do more finishes on a flat-sheened surface. Flat-sheened surfaces do not clean as well as those painted with a higher-sheened paint. The negative side of using higher gloss paint is that it magnifies all surface defects, such as nail pops, bad tape joints, lumps, dents and undulations. Flat paints hide flaws better than higher-sheened paints. For good washability, I recommend using a low-luster, satin or eggshell sheen on your walls. These will not magnify defects as much as a high-gloss sheen but still clean up very well. For additional protection, you can also clear-coat your surface with a clear sealer.

SEALERS

Most water-based glaze finishes, once they are cured (thirty days), are washable and are as durable as woodwork trim paint. If you want extra protection on a water-based finish, you can use either oil- or water-based sealers. The sealers come in a variety of sheens—flat, low-luster, semi-gloss and high-gloss. All water-based sealers are like paints in that the higher the sheen, the less flattening agents are in them. The more flattening agents there are, the milkier the paint film. All water-based sealers will create a slight bluish haze over darker colors which is more noticeable with a lower sheen. This bluish haze is often not noticed on mid to light colors. Be careful to use your sealers on warm, dry days. Coolness and higher humidity trap moisture under your sealer and cause even more hazing and irregular sheen problems. I very seldom seal my walls because they are usually durable enough after they cure for thirty days.

OIL-BASED PRODUCTS

For over twenty years of my career, I used an oil-based glazing recipe of 1 part oil-based paint, 1 part oil glazing medium and 1 part paint thinner. If I needed to extend my open time even more, I would add either boiled linseed oil or kerosene to my mixture. I would often use this mixture in small rooms during the winter months when I couldn't get a lot of ventilation. The client would come home and would almost fall over from the odor in the room. After working in the room for hours I didn't even know it smelled anymore! My clothes would reek from the solvents. When I came home no one wanted to be around me until I changed my clothes. I realized I needed to convert to a water-based paint system to avoid all the health issues involved with an oil-based system.

In the early 1990's I tried many different water-based glazes and did not like any of them. I was used to oils and I could not find a water-based system that allowed the working time and versatility of oil-based paints. Then I came across a water-based product line called Faux Effects. The same company manufactures Aqua Finishing Solutions. I fell in love with their glazes and their whole line of creative water-based products. They were nontoxic, with a working time that rivaled or surpassed oil-based formulas. They also offered unique finishes in a wide-ranging product line I could never attain with the oil products I had been using for over twenty years. Slowly, over two to three years, I weaned myself off my oil-based crutch and learned more and more about this fantastic line of paints. I truly feel that the Faux Effects line enabled me to work on a more creative level than ever before. And I believe that this manufacturer changed the whole field of decorative paint products for the faux finishing industry. I use a great number of their products to create many of my finishes.

SPECIALTY PAINTS & TEXTURIZING PRODUCTS

The book uses many different products from a wide range of manufacturers. Most of these are specialty items available through a network of manufacturers and distributors. In the Resource section in the back, I have listed the manufacturer and distributor of the products used in this book. I am also writing a brief description of each specialty product, what it is used for and if there is an available substitute product. If you change the products, you may not get the exact end result. If you know your paint products well and if there's a possibility to interchange products, try it. You may come up with something better than I did. All the Aqua Finishing Solutions and Pro Faux lines are designed to be compatible with everything in their respective lines.

AQUABOND

AquaBond is designed to be a durable wall trim and cabinet finish. This material is 100% acrylic and has superb bonding and sealing qualities that can easily be sanded to a smooth finish. AquaBond allows the most open time for your glazes when using AquaCreme and AquaGlaze. You can substitute this product with any low-sheen 100% acrylic paint, but they may not have the superb bonding properties that AquaBond does. If using AquaBond as a basecoat underneath a treatment, you may also use an eggshell or semi-glass latex paint as a substitute.

AQUACOLOR

AquaColor is a combination of non-organic color ground in a proprietary water-based resin. AquaColor can be used alone or as a color additive that can be mixed to tint any Aqua Finishing Solutions product. AquaColor is used alone for trompe l'oeil, stencil work, floor cloths and murals. You can substitute AquaColor with most artist acrylic paints such as Folk Art, Jo Sonja, etc.

AQUACREME

AquaCreme is a clear translucent glazing material that offers clarity, increased open time and durability. When used with AquaColor, AquaCreme allows you to execute detailed finishes using translucent layers of color. As a substitute you can use a translucent glazing material from another manufacturer such as Pro Faux, Modern Masters or Adicolor.

AQUAGLAZE

AquaGlaze is a water-based, slow drying medium used in combination with a good quality latex paint. Use the color charts at the paint store to tint the chosen latex paint and then combine with the glaze. There are many substitutes for this product available at most paint and hardware stores. Be careful because the open working time of glazes varies greatly. You will get the best open time using a specialty paint manufacturer like Pro Faux, Modern Masters, Poly Vine or Adicolor versus a paint manufacturer glaze.

AQUAGARD

AquaGard is a furniture quality, acrylic material formulated for use as a clear topcoat to increase the durability of a decorative finish or artwork. Substitute this product with any quality water-based clear sealer.

AQUASIZE

AquaSize is a glue-like material that works as the foundation coat in a two-part system designed to offer consistent results and a variety of crack patterns. I know of no other substitute for this material.

AQUASTONE

AquaStone is a textured material that contains actual marble dust suspended in an acrylic resin. It holds its shape when troweled on or texturized. It dries to a very hard, durable finish, yet it is very flexible for movement on walls. I have not tried any other product similar to AquaStone. If you substitute drywall mud, it will not be as durable or flexible as AquaStone. Plus you cannot easily stain over unpainted drywall mud like you can with AquaStone.

CRACKLEMATE

CrackleMate is a clear paint additive that transforms Aqua Finishing Solutions products and ordinary latex paints into a crackle medium that can be applied over AquaSize. I know of no substitute for this product.

DUTCH METAL

Dutch Metal is a high-hide liquid metal product that can be used for a variety of painting techniques. You can substitute this product with any water-based, liquid metal leafing product found in arts and crafts stores.

LIME SLAG

Lime Slag is a lime-based putty additive created for use with Faux Effects plasters and textured materials. There is no known substitute for Lime Slag.

LUSTERSTONE

LusterStone is a revolutionary architectural coating that produces beautiful reflective stone-like patterns. It is available in forty different colors. There is no known substitute for LusterStone.

METALGLOW

MetalGlow is a beautiful, lustrous paint that seems to glow from within. When properly applied, it can be used alone or as a basecoat for decorative glazing, stenciling and artistic embellishments. MetalGlow can be substituted with a wide range of water-based metallic paints available at a variety of art and craft stores.

PALETTE DECO

Palette Deco is a durable paste-like water-based product that can be applied in a variety of ways and does not need a protective topcoat.

PLASTERTEX

PlasterTex is a specially formulated textured material designed to produce a grained plaster finish. I know of no other substitute for this product.

ROLCO SLOW SET SIZE

This is an oil-based gilding varnish that is used to transfer leaf or foil products. You can substitute this product with any other slow setting oil-based gilding varnish.

SOFTEX

SofTex is a water-based material that is translucent and soft to the touch. It is used to create a variety of finishes and has excellent bonding and sound absorbing qualities. There is no known substitute for this product.

STAIN & SEAL

Stain & Seal is a water-based stain and seal gel which can be used for staining or antiquing and also as a tint for AquaCreme or AquaGlaze.

VENETIAN GEM

Venetian Gem is a synthetic, water-based plaster. Many substitutes are available from Behr, Pro Faux, Adicolor and Modern Masters.

PRO FAUX PLASTERS

Venetian Plaster, Metallic Waxes, Iridescent Waxes and Clear Satin Wax are only a part of a large decorative paint product line that Pro Faux distributes through a nationwide network. Substitute similar products from other specialty lines such as Aqua Finishing Solutions or Adicolor.

ADICOLOR PAINT PRODUCTS

Desiré is only one of many products that this paint company offers through a network of distributors nationwide. I know of no substitute for Desiré.

FONDO

Fondo is a lightly textured, fine-grained paint that Desiré will bond to. Substitute with any fine-grained or textured paint from Aqua Finishing Solutions, Pro Faux or another specialty paint manufacturer.

PRO TIPS

PRO TIP 1 Test Your Glaze
Always test any glaze, either latex or oil, to be sure its consistency and translucency are what you require.

PRO TIP 2 How to Thicken Glaze
If the glaze does not hold its design on the wall, you can thicken it by using more paint.

PRO TIP 3 How to Thin Glaze
If you can't see the wall color through the glaze, add more glazing medium, glazing extender or water to thin it.

PRO TIP 4 How Colorant Affects Glaze
The depth of glaze color is affected by how much colorant you put into the glaze. For a more translucent glaze, use less colorant.

PRO TIP 5 WARNING
When making up a glaze, do not use all your paint at once, in case you need to adjust the glaze's thickness or transparency.

PRO TIP 6 Check for the Correct Quantity
Once your glaze is right in all respects, make sure you have enough to finish the whole room.

PRO TIP 7 Keep Glaze from Thickening
All glazes, both oil and water, will thicken if the container is left open for about twelve hours. (The actual amount of time required will vary depending on the environment.) Seal your container of glaze to prevent this from happening.

PRO TIP 8 Consistency is Important
Consistency is critical while applying your glaze. If you want a nice even color, you will need to apply your glaze as evenly as possible. If you want an irregular finish, apply your glaze heavier in some areas and lighter in others.

GLAZES

In today's marketplace, there are many different manufacturers of water-based glazing mediums. The main purpose of a glazing medium is to extend the working open time of water-based paints and to make the paints more translucent so you can see through one layer of paint to another below. Each manufacturer makes their glazes differently, so you will need to experiment with them to see which you like best for yourself. I use a variety of glazes but the one I use most often when mixing my glaze with a latex-based paint is AquaGlaze. I usually use AquaCreme (a clear glazing medium) when I want a sheer glaze that I can custom color myself with either AquaColor (a pure liquefied 100% acrylic paint) or universal tinting agents.

I mostly work in the Cincinnati area, and my standard AquaGlaze mixture is 3–4 parts AquaGlaze to 1 part latex-based paint in the color of my choice. You may need to increase or decrease the amount of glazing medium you use in your mixture depending upon where you live. If you are in a cool, humid environment, you will need less glaze in your mix than if you are in a warmer and drier climate. My recipe works well for the Midwest.

I will usually tint AquaCreme up to the desired color by using AquaColor. When using AquaGlaze, the glazes tend to be a little more opaque than when you use the tinted AquaCreme. Therefore, I mostly use AquaGlaze on flat wall finishes and AquaCreme over dimensional textured surfaces.

When I custom-tint AquaCreme, I measure an exact amount of AquaCreme (say 8 ounces or 24 centiliters) and then I use a disposable metric syringe to measure 2cc of one color and 3cc of another or whatever the measurements may be. I can always repeat the mixing process in any volume over and over and repeatedly make the same color, just like a paint store mixing up their paints.

A quart of latex-based paint mixed with a gallon (4 liters) of AquaGlaze (which is a 1:4 ratio) will cover approximately 500 square feet (47 square meters) of wall space. A gallon (4 liters) of AquaCreme will cover approximately 400 square feet (37 square meters) of wall space over a non-dimensional finish. On a textured finish, however, the glaze tends to be pushed out further, which increases the square footage it will cover to approximately 600 square feet (56 square meters) per gallon (4 liters) of AquaCreme. When you tint AquaCreme, use a small amount of AquaColor or a lesser amount of universal colorant, which is a more concentrated pigment. When you tint AquaCreme, a little bit of color will keep your AquaCreme more sheer and translucent whereas a higher concentration of color will increase your opacity and depth of color.

STORAGE AND LABELING

All paints should be kept in a cool, dry area and never allowed to freeze. Do not store your paints in your garage unless it does not freeze in your part of the country. The rims of your paint cans should be kept clean so the lids will seal properly when reapplied. Use a felt-tip marker to label all cans of paint with the date, name of paint, paint formula if it's a computer-matched color or you made it yourself, what it was used for (basecoat on walls, trim color, etc.) and in what room it was used. In five years, if you need to touch up your walls for any reason, you will be very happy that you did this.

BRUSHES

In order to execute the best finish, you need to buy the best brushes you can afford. The better your brushes, the better your results. An inexpensive brush will not last long and will almost always give you an inferior look. If you take good care of your brushes and all the tools mentioned in this book, they will last for many years.

BRUSH SIZE

Your job will go a lot faster if you have a variety of brush sizes. Use the correct size brush for the area. If you are working around a door frame that is very close to the adjacent wall, don't try to smash a 4-inch (10cm) brush into that area. Instead, use a small artist's brush. Don't use a small 1-inch (25mm) brush to cut in your base or glaze coat around the large open areas in a room. Use a 2- to 4-inch (51mm to 10cm) brush.

BRUSH QUALITY

Quality brushes are hand-crafted from a variety of materials. Brushes used for water-based paints are usually made from synthetics like a nylon or polyester blend. Oil-based paint brushes are often made of pig or ox hair. Do not use a latex brush in an oil-based paint because the strong solvents may damage your brush. Likewise, do not use an oil brush in a water-based paint because the water will explode the natural hairs in the brush and ruin its fine quality. Make sure that your brush has a chiseled edge and will hold a fair amount of paint. Even high-quality brushes may shed hairs. It's a good practice to break in all new brushes by flicking the bristles back and forth until all the loose hairs have come out. The price of brushes often indicates the quality. Buy the best brushes you can afford and then experiment with different, less expensive brushes.

CHIP BRUSH

In the decorative painting field, I feel that the best all-purpose brush is the chip brush. It comes in a variety of sizes and is usually made of white China bristle (pig) hair. These brushes are very inexpensive ($0.79 up to $4.00, depending on size) and you can use them in latex and oil paints. I use them a lot in my own work, and when one becomes worn or damaged, I can get a new one for another $0.79. These brushes do tend to shed hairs when new, so be careful how and where you use them. When I first use a new chip brush, I flick the hairs back and forth to remove any loose hairs. I then use the chip brush as a pouncing brush to even out glaze along moldings and corners for two to three rooms. By then, the brush has lost whatever hairs it may lose, and I can use it to brush on my glazes or cut in a room, as well as a pouncing brush.

PAINT ROLLERS AND SLEEVES

My other favorite tool for applying glazes, textures or cutting in basecoats is the 4-inch (10cm) Whizz roller (see Resources). I often use two to four of these on a job. I have each product in a gallon (4 liter) bucket and use a little gallon (4 liter) paint grid inside the bucket to roll my paint off. This speeds up my production. These Whizz rollers have become indispensable to me. I use the Whizz Fab sleeve cover a lot or I sometimes use the foam sleeve to achieve a very smooth finish. When glazing large areas with one glaze color, I use either the Whizz Premium Gold Stripe roller cover or a ½-inch (13mm) lambskin roller sleeve. These sleeves clean up quickly and last a long time. For basecoats or larger glazing areas, use a 9-inch (23cm) roller frame with a ½-inch (13mm) nap lambskin cover. These hold a lot of material, do not spatter and clean up quickly. On large jobs I pour my base paint into 5-gallon (19 liter) buckets, use a 5-gallon (19 liter) bucket grid and roll our paint out of the 5-gallon (19 liter) bucket, which is another time saver.

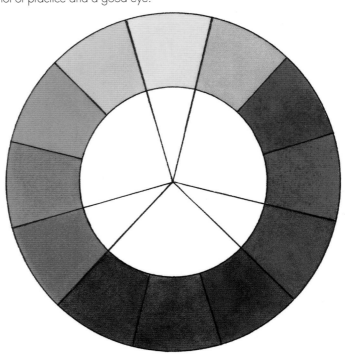

COLOR

Today, thanks to highly technical paint manufacturers such as Benjamin Moore, we can choose from a wide variety of paint colors that can be consistently reproduced. Also, with the use of the color-matching computer systems, we can get colors computer-matched and made for us just as easily as buying a standard paint color. This is a tremendous benefit if you need to make an exact color match from fabric, wallpaper or a custom paint mix for your project. You can also computer-match the dots of color in each one of the recipes in this book

CHOOSING A COLOR

Choose a color that relates well to the room conditions. You should take into consideration both natural and artificial lighting in the room as well as the room's furniture, carpet, pictures and fabrics. Always remember that darker colors in a room bring the walls in and are more intimate, while lighter colors recede so that the room appears more open.

Once you know something about the room you are painting, you are more likely to make a successful choice from a color card or a bundle of swatches. There is no better way to ensure you have chosen the correct color than painting a sample board. You can then move it around to see how the color looks under the room's varying light conditions.

The texture and sheen of the finish also affect the color. For example, you can create a beautiful decorative paint finish by using exactly the same shade of color but allowing one paint to be in a flat sheen and another to be in a gloss. You can paint walls in a stripe pattern this way. You can also rag, sponge or feather-dust them to create a beautiful, subtle finish much like damask material.

COMBINING COLORS

When it comes to combining colors in a decorative scheme, many people are hesitant. In combining colors, as in many other aspects of decoration, observation is important. Inspiration comes from successful color schemes you see in books and magazines and also from fabric patterns and paintings in the room in which you are working. Examples of good color combinations are everywhere. You should train yourself to look for interesting color combinations and then ask yourself what makes them work.

In recent history, there has been an endless variety of colors used in decorating. A desire for muted intense colors and metallics seems to be popular again. Although every decade has had its own particular colors that are in vogue, white and off-whites are persistent color themes.

COLOR MIXING

Despite the wide range of hues of ready-mixed paints available today, you can achieve a greater degree of subtlety and variety by mixing your own colors. Color mixing is something of an art and requires a lot of practice and a good eye.

If you are just learning about color theory, it is best to get a color wheel and practice making up different colors, varying these hues and values until you begin to understand what pigments it takes to create certain colors.

COLOR THEORY

Color theory is a very complex and intricate part of decorative painting. There are many books devoted especially to color theory, and they go into much more detail that I can in this book. For those who are new to color theory, I would recommend taking a class and reading books on that topic.

CREATIVITY

I have found over the years that my staff and I are so busy that if I do not plan time to become creative, it often never happens. So once a year, if not more often, my staff and I will go away to a major design city such as Chicago and look at what is new in color, fabrics and textures in the decorating field. Other years we will all attend a national convention such as SALI (see Resources) to see new products and ways to use them. We will collect samples, take photographs and write down ideas to use later. We will try to visit museums or art shows as well, and in the evenings we go out to good dinners and then hear live music or go see a play. We make it a fun, arts-filled three days. Our goal is to be inspired to create new techniques with our newfound knowledge. The more fun we can have, the more creative we

are later. As a team, we then decide on the new products we want to try and what other products we may need to restock. Once all the products are in (usually a week or so after our trip), we will schedule three play days in the studio to create our new ideas. We brainstorm and inspire each other. We also sweeten the pot a little and vote on our favorite pieces of each other's work. The artist with the piece that has the most votes wins a dinner out for two.

Each of us will make ten to twenty samples in these three days, for a total of seventy to one hundred new samples. We then plan a few months later to have a grand showing of our new collection for designers, architects and builders, to showcase our new work. On the following day, we open the show up to the general public for everyone to see what's new.

Even if you work alone, you can use this same idea. Network with friends who do decorative finishes as well, have fun, become inspired and feel the joy of creating. Use books such as this one for inspirational ideas, then gather all of your new products and share ideas with your friends.

This book includes finished techniques my staff and friends came up with. Rawhide (page 66) was created by David Texter, Micah Knockdown (page 130) by Micah Ballard, Autumn Leaves (page 114) by Greg and John from Pro Faux, Colette's Classic (page 62) by Colette Hayden, Penny Lane (page 126) by Kris Hampton, Sutherland Rainbow (page 122) by Jeff Sutherland and Shimmer & Lace (page 90) by Dave and Pam Schmidt.

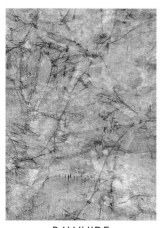

RAWHIDE

MICAH KNOCKDOWN

PENNY LANE

SUTHERLAND RAINBOW

AUTUMN LEAVES

COLETTE'S CLASSIC

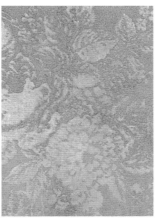

SHIMMER & LACE

On the following pages you'll find thirty unique faux finishes. All projects include lists of materials, preparation directions and special pro-tips that will give you "insider information" before you even start the project. And, of course, each technique is shown with easy-to-follow, step-by-step instruction. Most projects can be completed in three to four steps.

There is something for everyone—from the seasoned professional to the first-time home decorator. Everything is here to help you create gorgeous faux finishes in your home!

PROJECT ONE
ONE-COLOR CHEESECLOTH

This finish is so universal that it can be used with any decor in any room. Just change the color to fit your needs if these colors don't work for you. This is a great finish for a beginning faux finisher to do because of its simplicity. An advanced finisher will use this in their "bread and butter" techniques, because of its ease and high profitability.

Home of Kim & Dan Watkoske

MATERIALS

paint tray

9-inch (23cm) roller with ½ inch (13mm) nap lambskin sleeve

cheesecloth

AquaCreme

AquaColors:

  Earth Brown

  Ochre Yellow

ochre yellow latex paint

COLOR PALETTE

ochre yellow
eggshell
latex
paint

Aquacreme
tinted with
Earth Brown
and
Ochre Yellow

PREP

This finish can be applied over any latex-based paint in an eggshell or semi-gloss sheen. I recommend applying two solid basecoats in a 100% acrylic eggshell paint. This allows you the longest working time for your glaze.

PRO TIPS

PRO TIP 1 **Use Cheesecloth for Application**
Use laundered cheesecloth for this application. The reason for this is that the laundered cheesecloth has fewer fibers that will fall out during the working process.

PRO TIP 2 **How to Hold the Cheesecloth**
Use multiple pieces of cheesecloth at one time and make a loose puff ball. When using the cheesecloth ball on the wall, always keep your hand on the top part of it. This avoids having your fingertips print an image on the surface.

PRO TIP 3 **Working with the Glaze**
If your working area is drying too fast for you to remove the glaze, try working in a smaller area. You can also mist your working area with water prior to applying AquaCreme. Another way to increase the working time of AquaCreme is to add a small amount of AquaExtender to your glaze mix. The more extender you add to your glaze mix, the more your working time is increased.

▪▪ STEP**ONE**

Apply your basecoats in the color of your choice. (We used an ochre yellow.) Allow to dry a minimum of four to six hours, though twenty-four to forty-eight hours is even better. The longer you allow your basecoat to dry, the more working time you will have later when applying AquaCreme.

▪▪ STEP**TWO**

Mix the AquaCreme with AquaColors Earth Brown and Ochre Yellow to your own desired depth of color. Apply this glaze in a medium density in an approximately 3' x 3' (1m x 1m) area, leaving your outside edges irregular and being careful not to create any geometric shapes such as rectangles or squares. This will make the transition areas less visible. Roll your glaze on with a ½-inch (13mm) nap lambskin sleeve on a 9-inch (23cm) wide roller when doing this step.

■■ STEP**THREE**

Remove excess glaze using your puffed-up cheesecloth
with a firm pressure and a slight twist to your hand—
allowing the cheesecloth to slide slightly on the surface
in a hit-skip motion. Continue this process around
the room, working your wet edge in and out of the
previously glazed areas. *(See Pro Tips 1, 2 and 3.)*

FINISHED TECHNIQUE

FINISHED TECHNIQUE

PROJECT TWO
TWO-COLOR CHEESECLOTH

This treatment is basically the same as the one-color cheesecloth finish in its benefits for beginner to advanced faux finishers. The use of the second color adds more movement and dimensionality to the walls than just using one color. Adding the second color also incorporates more colors from the room's palette into the wall finish all in one step. Vary the basecoat and glaze colors to go with your own decor or simply use the ones here if they work for you.

The Biedermann Home

MATERIALS

Aquabond:
  Off-White
two 4-inch (10cm) Whizz rollers
AquaCreme
misting bottle
cheesecloth
paint tray

COLOR PALETTE

Off-White
AquaBond

Color-tinted
AquaCreme

Color-tinted
AquaCreme

PREP

For the basecoat on this treatment, we used two full coats of Off-White AquaBond. This treatment works best on smooth surfaces.

PRO TIPS

PRO TIP 1 Launder the Cheesecloth
Use laundered cheesecloth for this application. The reason is that the laundered cheesecloth has fewer fibers that will fall out during the working process.

PRO TIP 2 How to Hold the Cheesecloth
Use multiple pieces of cheesecloth at one time and make a loose puff ball. When using the cheesecloth ball on the wall, always keep your hand on the top part of it. This avoids having your fingertips print an image on the surface. (See photos below.)

PRO TIP 3 Working with the Glaze
If your work area is drying too fast for you to remove the glaze, try working in a smaller area. You can also mist your working area with water prior to applying AquaCreme. Another way to increase the working time of the AquaCreme is to add a small amount of AquaExtender to your glaze mix. The more extender you put into your glaze mix, the more your working time is increased.

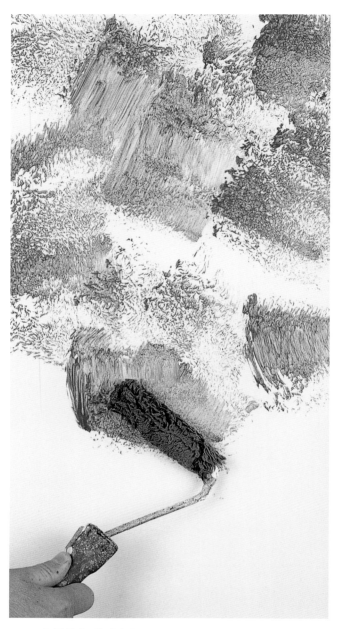

■■ STEP**ONE**

Working in a 2' x 2' (½m x ½m) area, use your 4-inch (10cm) Whizz roller to apply one color irregularly over 60% of your working area. The amount of material on the surface should be a medium density.

■■ STEP**TWO**

Apply your second glaze color with a different Whizz roller over 60% of your working area. While the first glaze is still wet you want to aim at your negative areas—to fill them in—while slightly overlapping your first color as well. It is OK to have about 5% of your background color peeking through in small areas.

■■ STEP**THREE**

With a slight twisting motion of your hand, pat the surface firmly with your cheesecloth to even out the glaze—being careful not to let your fingerprints telegraph through the cheesecloth. *(See Pro Tips 1, 2 and 3.)*

FINISHED TECHNIQUE

FINISHED TECHNIQUE

PROJECT THREE
NO-GLAZE GLAZE

This may be the easiest finish in the book for a beginning faux finisher, yet it is one an advanced finisher can use for a quick, easy and inexpensive technique. I have this treatment in my own home in my master bedroom and sitting room. Because of its subtle textural look, this can be used in any room. If the colors used are too strong for you, lighten them up and make them more neutral for a soft, pretty, mottled finish. For example, try the colors from the Two-Color Ralston technique (Project 4) but use them to do this finish.

Home of Bryan & Kimberly Carlisle

MATERIALS

AquaBond:

  Khaki

one quart of each latex paint:

  purple

  russet

  green

paint tray

three 1-gallon (4 liter) buckets

cotton sheeting

protective gloves

COLOR PALETTE

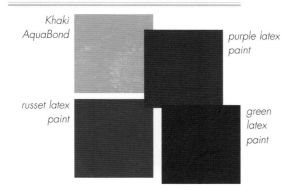

Khaki AquaBond

russet latex paint

purple latex paint

green latex paint

PREP

Make sure your walls are in sound condition. Fill any nail pops, dents, cracks, etc. prior to applying your basecoat of paint. This finish works best on smooth surfaces.

PRO TIPS

PRO TIP 1 Tips for Beginners

This is a great treatment for a beginner, because it is a positive application technique where you don't have to worry about keeping an edge of your paint wet. Therefore, you can start and stop anywhere in the process and not have a problem. It's an extremely fast and fun technique.

PRO TIP 2 WARNING!

For the first twenty-four hours this finish stays extremely soft because of the high water content in the glaze. Therefore, the first coat will be reactivated and partially removed by the second coat if you apply your second glaze color on it within twenty-four hours. If you want to do all three glaze coats in a day you can, but you must be aware that the finish will be a different color than if you allow each coat to dry twenty-four hours in between..

PRO TIP 3 Be Consistent with the Application

After a few minutes your rag will start to dry out and you will have to re-saturate it with your color again. What you're looking for on the wall is to keep the same varying color value everywhere. As in all faux finishes, consistency of the treatment is critical, so always look for varying contrasts and correct them as you go along.

▪▪▪ STEP**ONE**

Apply two basecoats of the Khaki AquaBond or use a 100% acrylic-based eggshell paint computer-matched to the color shown in the color palette to use as your base color.

▪▪▪ STEP**TWO**

Mix the purple latex color with 150% water to the volume of paint in a gallon (4 liter) bucket. Basically, what you're doing at this point is making a very sheer water-based stain of the color.

Wearing your protective gloves, saturate a piece of cotton sheeting with the mixture and ring out all the excess. Then, with a patting, twisting, skipping hand motion, cover 60% of your surface area. Allow to dry, which usually happens very quickly. *(See Pro Tips 1 and 3.)*

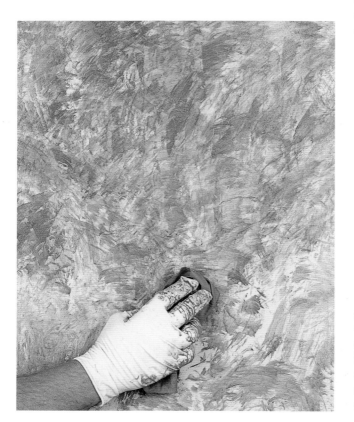

▪▪▪ STEP**THREE**

Apply the russet color in the same fashion as you did the purple but deliberately aim for the negative areas and overlap into the purple areas. Allow to dry. *(See Pro Tip 2.)*

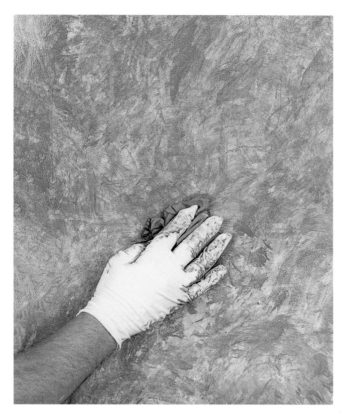

■■ STEP**FOUR**

Mix up the green color as you did the first two colors. Saturate your rag and remove all excess. This time, rub the rag onto a 2' x 2' (½m x ½m) section of your working area with a broad circular motion. Do a slight pat over 100% of this area while the glaze is still wet. Continue around the room in the same manner.

FINISHED TECHNIQUE

FINISHED TECHNIQUE

PROJECT FOUR
TWO-COLOR RALSTON

I sell this particular finish more often than any other technique. It is not always done in these colors because I am always trying to match the colors of the room I am working in. Most people enjoy this soft finish because of its universal look which can go with any décor, from traditional to contemporary. Sometimes people wonder how I come up with names for finishes. This was named after Dave Schmidt's client the first time he did it—the Ralstons.

Home of Tony Watson & Sherri Lanter

MATERIALS

AquaBond:

  Off-White

one quart (.9 liter) khaki latex paint

one quart (.9 liter) taupe latex paint

AquaGlaze

two 4-inch (10cm) Whizz rollers

two 1-gallon (4 liter) buckets

two 1-gallon (4 liter) bucket screens

cotton sheeting

COLOR PALETTE

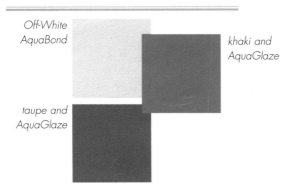

Off-White AquaBond

khaki and AquaGlaze

taupe and AquaGlaze

PRO TIPS

PRO TIP 1 **Use a Cotton Percale Rag to Apply**
I prefer using cotton percale sheeting when I am doing a rag finish such as this one. (A thread count of over 700 for my picky clients is ideal!)

PRO TIP 2 **How to Hold the Rag**
Make sure you bunch up the rag into a loose puff ball and hold your hand on the top of the rag—similar to the way you held the cheesecloth. See Pro Tip 2 on page 27.

PRO TIP 3 **Blend your Colors**
It is important for your colors to start to blend a little in this process. I want these colors to mingle and it's OK if they touch each other, so don't be afraid to let them overlap.

PRO TIP 4 **Mix your Colors in a Large Bucket**
On a job we will mix our colors in a gallon bucket (4 liters) and then use a gallon (4 liters) bucket screen with our Whizz roller. We work right out of the bucket, and off-load our roller onto the bucket screen before rolling the glaze on the wall.

PRO TIP 5 **Product Preference**
If I have the choice of background paints to use, many times I will select a brand called AquaBond, which comes in a wide variety of colors. AquaBond is a 100% acrylic paint that allows superior open time for my glazing applications.

STEP**ONE**

Basecoat your surface with two full coats of Off-White AquaBond.

STEP**TWO**

Using your 4-inch (10cm) Whizz roller, apply your first glaze color (I used 4 parts AquaGlaze to 1 part khaki latex paint) irregularly over 60% of your 2' x 2' (½m x ½m) working area. The amount of glaze material on the surface should be a medium density.

STEP**THREE**

While your first glaze color is still wet, apply a second glaze color (4 parts AquaGlaze to 1 part taupe latex paint) with a different Whizz roller over 60% of your surface area. You want to aim at the negative areas—to fill them in—while slightly overlapping your first color. It is OK to have about 5% of your background color peeking through in small areas. *(See Pro Tips 3 and 4.)*

▪▪■ STEP**FOUR**

Take your loosely balled cotton sheeting and, with a firm pressure, pat the surface with a slight twist and skimming motion to your hand. You want the colors to blend together in some areas and maintain their individual color in other areas. Continue working around the room in this manner.

(See Pro Tips 1 and 2.)

FINISHED TECHNIQUE

FINISHED TECHNIQUE

PROJECT FIVE
LINEN STRIE

This linen strie was created as a soft, soothing finish to complement the elegant surroundings of this award-winning master bedroom suite. Linen strie can be used in dining rooms, bedrooms, foyers, bathrooms or anywhere a classic, subtle, elegant finish is required. My friend and co-worker, Joe Taylor, helped me come up with this finish.

Photo courtesy of Robin Victor Goetz

MATERIALS

paint tray

9-inch (23cm) roller and ½-inch (13mm) nap lambskin sleeve

pole extension

AquaGlaze

strie or 4-inch (10cm) chip brush

rags

plumb line or laser level

walkboard or ladders

off-white eggshell latex paint

butter gold latex paint

COLOR PALETTE

off-white
eggshell
latex

off-white
and
AquaGlaze

butter gold
and
AquaGlaze

PREP

Make sure your walls are in sound condition. Fill any nail pops, dents, cracks, etc. prior to applying your basecoat of paint. This finish works best on smooth surfaces.

PRO TIPS

PRO TIP 1 Applying your Basecoat
When applying your basecoat on the wall, cut in as tightly as you can with your roller to all edges. The reason for this is that cutting in with a wide brush often creates a striated mark that is contrary to the direction of the decorative strie pattern.

PRO TIP 2 Using a Pole Extension
I find it easy to tape the brush to a paint pole extension — the one I use is 16" (41cm) — or one that is adjustable in varying lengths. That way I do not need to use a ladder to strie the wall.

PRO TIP 3 Keeping your Lines Straight
Keeping my strie lines vertical is like a Zen art — if you think too much and overcompensate, your lines won't stay straight. So to keep them as straight as possible, I use a laser beam from a laser level I set up and then move it along the wall as I finish each section. If you don't want to rent or invest in a laser level, you can use a plumb line and move it as you go.

PRO TIP 4 Paint with One Continuous Movement
It is best to run your strie in one long continuous movement — cleaning your brush after each pass with your rag to remove excess glaze from the brush.

PRO TIP 5 Painting your Horizontal Stripes
It's easiest to do your horizontal stripes at ceiling level by setting up a walkboard, which will place you at the appropriate height. Once you become proficient at this technique, just move a ladder down the wall and work on the ladder.

PRO TIP 6 WARNING!
The nature of doing a hand-painted strie is that it creates a slightly different demarcation of the strie at the ceiling line and baseboard, where the strie brush starts and stops. This is the beauty of this hand-painted finish. Some people find this bothersome. To compensate for this problem — if it is apparent — drag a piece of course steel wool or the strie brush through the glaze in these areas for a few inches before you strie that whole area with the brush.

■■ STEP**ONE**

Apply two solid coats of eggshell latex paint. You may choose not to do the basecoat yourself and hire a professional (or your children— whoever is cheaper!). In my case, the professional is cheaper.

■■ STEP**TWO**

Mix 1 part of your butter gold color with 4 parts AquaGlaze. Apply this in a medium density on the surface in a swath about 2' (½m) wide by the height of your room. Then, take your 4-inch (10cm) chip brush *(See Pro Tip 2)* and, with a medium to firm pressure at a 45° angle to the wall, drag your brush to create the vertical striated marks. *(See Pro Tips 3 and 4.)*

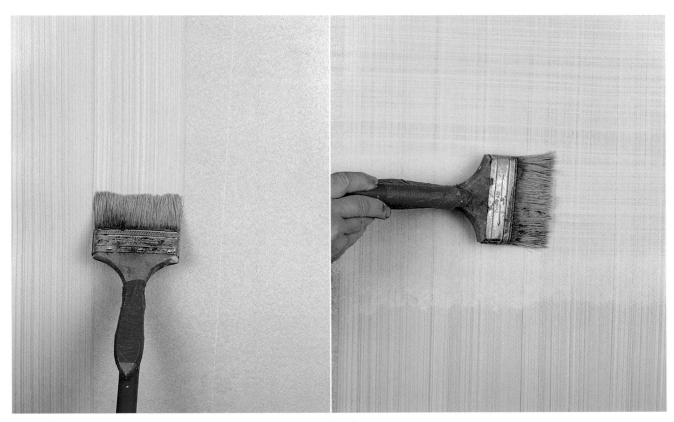

▪▪ STEP **THREE**

Often, we do vertical strie like you have just completed and that is the final technique. But to create the look of linen, we need to do another step, the horizontal strie. Mix your off-white color with 4 parts AquaGlaze to 1 part paint. Apply your glaze using a 9-inch (23cm) roller in a swath 2-feet (½m) wide by the length of your wall. Start the horizontal stripe at the top of your ceiling and work down toward the baseboard. Continue this process around the room, working on one full wall at a time. *(See Pro Tips 5 and 6.)*

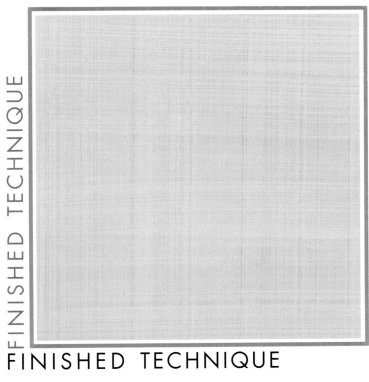

FINISHED TECHNIQUE

FINISHED TECHNIQUE

PROJECT SIX
PARCHMENT

This technique is Dave Schmidt's most requested finish and is in my top three most often requested techniques. The colors used in this exact finish have been very successful because of their rich warmth and beauty, like Autumn colors. These colors look especially beautiful against the natural cherry wood tones of cabinetry and mahogany furniture in the room. This treatment is often used in kitchens, bathrooms and dining rooms. We even used these exact colors in a billiard room in a manor estate in Northern England on one of our international teaching workshops.

Homearama 2003, Hensley Homes, Henry T. Vittetoe III, Designer

MATERIALS

2-inch (51mm) chip brush

AquaBond:

  Woody Yellow

cotton rags

AquaCreme

AquaColor:

  Van Dyke Brown

  Dark Brown

  French Red

low-luster latex paint:

  green

  rust

4-inch (10cm) Whizz roller

paint tray

9-inch (23cm) roller and ½-inch (13mm) nap lambskin sleeve

badger brush

COLOR PALETTE

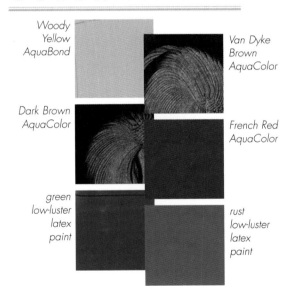

Woody Yellow AquaBond

Van Dyke Brown AquaColor

Dark Brown AquaColor

French Red AquaColor

green low-luster latex paint

rust low-luster latex paint

PREP

Apply two full-coverage basecoats of AquaBond Woody Yellow or a 100% acrylic latex in a matching color. This project works best on a smooth wall surface. (See Pro Tip 1.)

PRO TIPS

PRO TIP 1 **How Much AquaBond Will You Need?**
One gallon (4 liters) of Woody Yellow AquaBond will cover 400 sq. ft. (37 sq.m).

PRO TIP 2 **How Much Latex Paint Will You Need?**
One quart (.9 liter) of latex paint, used this way, will cover 400 sq. ft. (37 sq.m). (One quart of each color will do most average rooms.)

PRO TIP 3 **Watch Your Time**
Because the movement is mostly created by a damp rag, the colors remain soft and do not quickly dry hard. You need to be careful to stay in sequence with the drying time with each area that you work. If you allow the green in one area to dry overnight and you've only allowed it to dry in another area for two hours, for example, your red color will re-activate and remove the softer area (which has dried for less time).

PRO TIP 4 **How Much AquaCreme Will You Need?**
One quart (.9 liter) of AquaCreme will cover 150 sq. ft. (14 sq.m).

▪▪ STEP**ONE**

Using a 2-inch (51mm) chip brush, or 4-inch (10cm) Whizz roller, apply the green low-luster latex paint straight from the can in random splotches. Look for varying sizes of splotches to be contained within a 1' x 1' (31cm x 31cm) working space. Do not allow paint to dry. *(See Pro Tip 2.)*

▪▪ STEP**TWO**

While the paint is still wet, soften the color using a wet, well wrung-out rag (if the rag is too wet, the color may bead up or run). Wad the rag loosely in your hand and pounce the surface N-S-E-W with a hit-skip motion. Your goal is to break up and soften the color and to remove any hard brush or roller marks. What you are ultimately looking for is to create three varying values of your green color—light, medium and dark. Complete this step around the room.

▪▪ STEP**THREE**

Repeat steps 1 and 2 using the rust latex low-luster paint. Work in and over the first green color to even out values of light and dark areas with a combination of both colors. When applying the second color, aim for the lighter areas with your brush or roller then push out the paint with your damp rag to even out the values. Let dry.

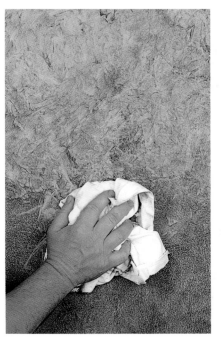

■■ STEP**FOUR**

Mix your AquaCreme with 50% Dark Brown, 30% Van Dyke Brown and 20% French Red. Apply this to your surface using the 4-inch (10cm) Whizz roller in a small working area, approximately 2' x 2' (½m x ½m). *(See Pro Tip 4.)*

■■ STEP**FIVE**

Take a dry rag and break up the glaze.

■■ STEP**SIX**

While the glaze is still wet, use your badger brush to soften the glaze—blurring the edges while your glaze is wet. Then continue steps 4, 5 and 6 around the room for 100% coverage.

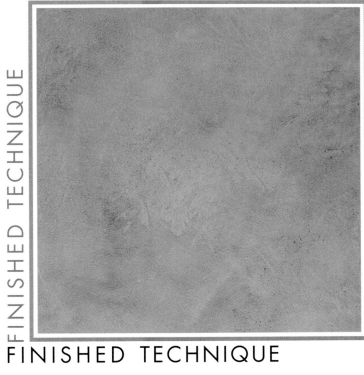

FINISHED TECHNIQUE

FINISHED TECHNIQUE

PROJECT SEVEN
EMBOSSED STENCILING

This treatment is perfect to use over any area that has surface imperfections, such as nail pops, dings, dents, cracks, bad drywall or walls torn up from wallpaper removal. Because of the varying dimensionality of this finish, the damaged areas just melt into the final look. Using any single overlay stencil, you can create this classic textured surface that works well in any room. (The finish photo on the left is in a different colorway than the room photo below.)

Home of Giorgio & Catherine Siracusa

MATERIALS

AquaColor:

French Red

Earth Brown

Yellow Ochre

Eggplant

Dark Brown

AquaStone

AquaCreme

9-inch (23cm) roller
with ⅜-inch (10mm)
to ½-inch (13mm)
nap lambskin sleeve

Royal Design Studio stencil:
Fleur de Lis (or single overlay
stencil of your choice)paint tray

6-inch (15cm) drywall
taping blade

misting bottle

two 4-inch (10cm) chip brushes

two 2-inch (5cm) chip brushes

cotton rags

100-grit sandpaper

COLOR PALETTE

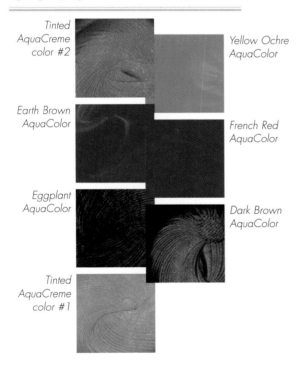

Tinted
AquaCreme
color #2

Yellow Ochre
AquaColor

Earth Brown
AquaColor

French Red
AquaColor

Eggplant
AquaColor

Dark Brown
AquaColor

Tinted
AquaCreme
color #1

PREP

This technique can be applied over any flat or eggshell
latex paint in a light-value color. The AquaStone has a lot
of Titanium White in it, so it has very good opacity.
This treatment is great on areas that have surface
imperfections (See Pro Tips 1 and 2) because the dimensional finish will hide a majority of problems. This
treatment is also suitable over existing wallpaper that is
still applied soundly to the surface area. (See page 10.)

PRO TIPS

PRO TIP 1 **Use on Imperfect Walls**
Because of the dimensionality of this finish, it is perfect to use
over badly damaged walls. This treatment will hide a
multitude of sins, such as torn-up walls, nail pops, stress
cracks, dings and dents from children's toys.

PRO TIP 2 **About AquaStone**
AquaStone is made of marble dust impregnated into an
acrylic polymer. It is extremely durable and easy to
maintain and keep clean. Because it is an acrylic product, it
will also allow moisture to flow in and out. It is an excellent
product to use in high-moisture-content areas such as
bathrooms and kitchens.

PRO TIP 3 **Applying AquaStone**
With the skip trowel technique, if you don't like an area, you
can remove it by holding your blade at a 90° angle to the
surface and, with a firm pressure, scraping off the
AquaStone. Then reapply the AquaStone in the negative
area, using the skip trowel technique. You are trying to
create a series of high and low spots with the AquaStone in
an interesting compositional format. Even though this step
may not be 100% hardened, it forms a crust on top but is soft
underneath. Apply the embossed stencils but don't press
down too hard in the process, unless the AquaStone is fully
dried and hard.

PRO TIP 4 **No Need to Clean Your Stencils**
It is seldom necessary to clean your stencils off while doing
this process. When the stencil is fully loaded with AquaStone,
place it into its new position and use the excess material on
the stencil to tack it into place. Then apply more material to
emboss the stencil again.

▪▪ STEP**ONE**

Roll on a medium-density coat of AquaStone that's been diluted 10% with water. Use your roller in a cross-hatch pattern with a light-to-medium pressure to apply the material evenly. Work in small sections, blending the material in and out from one area to another until the room is complete. Use a 9-inch (23cm) roller frame with a ⅜-inch (10mm) to ½-inch (13mm) lambskin nap sleeve to apply material. Allow the material to dry about one to two hours.

▪▪ STEP**TWO**

This next step uses a "skip-trowel" technique created by using a 6-inch (15cm) drywall taping blade. Dilute your AquaStone 10%–20% with water. Place a medium amount on one side of your blade. Hold your blade at a 25° angle to your surface. With a light pressure and a crescent-shaped movement, allow your material to skip across the surface and catch in some areas but not in others. Complete all around the room, working wet-into-wet, then allow to dry fully. It usually takes four to six hours for the AquaStone to dry *(See Pro Tip 3.)*

▪▪ STEP**THREE**

Use any single overlay stencil of your choice. You can apply your stencils randomly or in a perfect drop-match pattern. *(See Pro Tip 1, Embedded Stenciling on page 51.)* It is faster and easier to use your eyes and create a random pattern.

Place a small amount of the diluted AquaStone onto the drywall taping blade and, while holding it at a 45° angle to your surface, scrape AquaStone into 100% of the stencil. This will allow the stencil to tack itself into place. Once this is done, immediately apply more AquaStone on top of the stencil so it is raised about ⅛-inch (3mm) above the stencil.

▪▪ STEP**FOUR**

Now remove the stencil by pulling it straight up, so as not to disturb the raised stencil image. Repeat this process around the room and allow your raised stencils to fully dry and harden. Usually this takes four to six hours. *(See to Pro Tip 4.)*

■ ■ ■ STEP **FIVE**

Mist a 2' x 2' (½m x ½m) working surface with water. Apply the first premixed AquaCreme glaze color (color #1 in the color palette on page 47). I mixed together AquaColors French Red, Earth Brown and Ochre Yellow. Use a 2-inch (5cm) or 4-inch (10cm) chip brush to apply the AquaCreme randomly over 50% of the surface. Scrub the glaze into the texture in a varying pattern of large, medium and small areas.

■ ■ ■ STEP **SIX**

While the AquaCreme is still damp, lightly mist your working area again with water. Then apply your second premixed AquaCreme glaze color (color #2 in the color palette on page 47). I used AquaColors Eggplant, Dark Brown and a touch of French Red mixed together for this step. Use a clean 2-inch (5cm) or 4-inch (10cm) chip brush to apply the AquaCreme randomly over 50% of the surface. Scrub the glaze into the texture in a varying pattern of large, medium and small areas. Focus on filling all of the existing negative areas and blend into your transition areas, overlapping some of your first color.

■ ■ ■ STEP **SEVEN**

While your glazed area is slightly damp, take a balled-up cotton rag and remove the glaze from the high areas of the finish with a medium pressure. Continue this process— steps 4, 5, 6 and 7—around the room. Allow to dry.

■ ■ ■ STEP **EIGHT**

Take a piece of 100-grit sandpaper and lightly sand the tops of the design to reveal a small amount of the white AquaStone below. This will give more dimensionality to your finish and add a slightly aged look.

FINISHED TECHNIQUE

FINISHED TECHNIQUE

PROJECT EIGHT
EMBEDDED STENCILING

This texture, though slightly dimensional, is relatively flat to the touch when completed. Its elegance comes from the usage of the matte-sheened PlasterTex and the higher gloss Palette Deco used for the stencil images. From some angles, the light reflects off the Palette Deco and it is very noticeable, yet from a different angle with less light reflection, the stenciled images meld into the background wall. This allows the stencil images to shimmer and move with light as your eye travels around the room. This is a slight variation on a finish I learned from my friend Melanie Royal. If you like this finish, Melanie has many other great ideas in her own books and videos. (See Resources in the back of the book.)

Photo courtesy of Ron Kolb, Exposures Unlimited

MATERIALS

PlasterTex

"Leon Neon" stipple brush

paint tray

9-inch (23cm) roller with ⅜-inch (10mm) to ½-inch (13mm)
    nap lambskin sleeve

6-inch (15cm) drywall taping blade

Royal Design Studio stencil:

    Renaissance Tile Series 1

    (or single overlay stencil of your choice)

Palette Deco:

    Pearl

misting bottle

AquaCreme

AquaColor:

    Earth Brown

spray adhesive

COLOR PALETTE

Earth Brown
AquaColor

PREP

This finish can be applied over any flat or eggshell latex paint in a light-value color. The PlasterTex has a lot of white titanium in it, so it has very good opacity. This treatment is very good to use on areas that have minor surface imperfections—because this dimensional finish will hide the majority of those problems. This treatment is also suitable to put over existing wallpaper that is still applied soundly to the surface area (see page 10).

PRO TIPS

PRO TIP 1 Using a Drop-Match Pattern
When doing a perfect drop-match pattern you will need to know the exact height and width of your walls. I will always start my design on the most visible wall and base all other measurements from that wall. The other given measurement is the size of my stencil. In a perfect drop-match pattern, all mathematical distances between the stencils are constant.

PRO TIP 2 Using Spray Adhesive
You can use spray adhesive to help adhere your stencils flat to the surface to avoid the Palette Deco material bleeding through to the PlasterTex. You may need to clean off the stencils periodically on the front and back as you work.

PRO TIP 3 Number of Stencils Needed
I find it best to have a minimum of three stencils for this project and I prefer to have six. The reason for this is that it helps me see my composition as I apply the stencils in their appropriate areas. I also use blue tape to indicate where I want my next stencil to be.

PRO TIP 4 Working with the Glaze
When working your glaze from section to section, start slightly away from your last area. Off load the "Neon Leon" with a firm pressure. As the quantity of material decreases in your brush, use a lighter pressure and fade into your transition area. Make sure you can see NO transition.

■■■ STEP**ONE**

Roll on a thin-to-medium density coat of PlasterTex that has been diluted 10% to 20% with water. Use your roller in a cross-hatch pattern with a light-to-medium pressure to apply the material evenly. On a job site, we will use a 9-inch (23cm) roller with a ⅜-inch (10mm) to ½inch (13mm) nap lambskin sleeve to apply this material. Allow the material in this area to dry to a soft firmness while you are rolling on new material.

■■■ STEP**TWO**

Holding the 6-inch (15cm) drywall taping blade parallel to the surface, knock down the PlasterTex while it is still softly firm, using a soft pressure. It is best to move your blade in small crescent-shaped strokes to remove the roller marks and flatten the peaks of the PlasterTex, while still allowing the material to have highs and lows. Repeat steps 1 and 2, working in and out of each area while moving around the entire room. Once steps 1 and 2 are done in the entire area, allow your work to dry to a hard firmness.

■■■ STEP**THREE**

Holding your blade at a 45° angle to your surface, start out with a light pressure to scrape the surface, which will reveal the sand particles in the PlasterTex. As the material becomes drier and firmer, you can use a much harder pressure for this process.

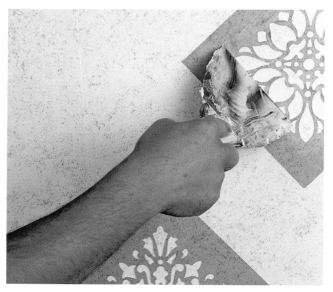

■■■ STEP**FOUR**

For this step, you can use any single overlay stencil of your choice. Apply your stencils either randomly or in a perfect drop-match pattern, as I did in this dining room. It is faster and easier to just use your eye and create a random pattern.

Take a small amount of your Pearl Palette Deco onto your drywall taping blade while holding it at a 75° angle. Scrape firmly and smoothly over 100% of your entire stencil. Continue placing your stencils around the room and allow the Palette Deco to dry fully.

▪▪ STEP**FIVE**

Mist your surface lightly with water in a 4' x 4' (1m x 1m) area.

▪▪ STEP**SIX**

Tint your AquaCreme to the desired shade. I used AquaCreme tinted with Earth Brown AquaColor for this technique. Apply a small amount of AquaCreme to the bottom of your "Neon Leon", then apply it to your PlasterTex wall, working in large circles to even out your glaze consistency on the wall. You can finesse your glaze with small circular motions. The glaze will absorb more on your PlasterTex areas than it will on your Palette Deco areas, which will act as a resist like the wax in batik painting does. Continue this process around the room, working from wet edge to wet edge of the glaze to avoid lap lines. *(See Pro Tip 4.)*

FINISHED TECHNIQUE

FINISHED TECHNIQUE

PROJECT NINE
DIMENSIONAL KNOCKDOWN WITH STENCILING

Dimensional Knockdown can also hide many defects, similar to the skip-trowel technique (see page 48). One difference is that the finish is not as rough and 3-D as with skip-trowel so it is easier to keep clean. That is why I chose this technique for the texture on this range hood. The raised stenciled border helps create a little more interest and defines the architecture of the hood. This treatment can be used on any surface in any room to add texture and color.

Home of Mr. & Mrs. Christopher Schweikert

MATERIALS

AquaStone

protective gloves

6-inch (15cm) drywall taping blade

Royal Design Studio stencil:

  Fleur de Lis

  (or single overlay stencil of your choice)

AquaCreme

"Leon Neon" stipple brush

AquaColor:

  Dark Brown

misting bottle

COLOR PALETTE

Dark Brown
AquaColor

PREP

This technique can be applied over any flat or eggshell latex paint in a light-value color. AquaStone has a lot of white titanium in it, so it has very good opacity. This treatment is very good to use on areas that have surface imperfections—because the dimensional finish will hide the majority of the problems. This treatment is also suitable to put over existing wallpaper that is still applied soundly to the surface area.

PRO TIPS

PRO TIP 1 Fixing Peaks and Knockdowns
If you have an area you don't like after you've knocked it down, peak it back up with your gloved hand and then use your drywall blade to knock it back down again.

PRO TIP 2 How to Hold Your Drywall Blade
Use your drywall blade at a 25° angle to the surface and scrape off the peaks on the AquaStone prior to stenciling.

PRO TIP 3 Checking the Raised AquaStone
A good way to know if you have enough of the raised AquaStone is to check that you only barely see the outline of the stencil below.

PRO TIP 4 Checking Your Glaze
A minute or so after you have glazed your stencil area, look back at it to make sure there are no drips or runs coming out of the stencil.

■■ STEP**ONE**

Dilute the AquaStone 10%–15% with water. Apply a protective glove to your hand and then, working in a 2' x 2' (½m x ½m) area, swirl the AquaStone onto your surface in a smooth layer, which is raised about ⅛-inch (10mm) off the sur-face—covering 100% of the working area.

■■ STEP**TWO**

While the AquaStone is still wet, splay your hand and pat it firmly while twisting your hand to create highs and lows in the AquaStone.

■■ STEP**THREE**

While the AquaStone is still wet, hold your 6-inch (15cm) drywall blade parallel to the surface and, with a light pressure, knock down the peaks of the AquaStone in small crescent-shaped areas. Continue this process around the room, working wet-into-wet, once all areas are fully dry. *(See Pro Tip 1.)*

■■ STEP**FOUR**

Sometimes I will take a stencil and mask out areas that I don't want to use. On this project, I only wanted a border to be raised on the front of the range hood soffit. So I masked out the parts of the stencil I didn't want. Apply a small amount of your AquaStone onto your drywall blade and scrape it over the stencil—covering 100%. This will tack the stencil into place and, once this is done, apply a ⅛-inch (10mm) layer of AquaStone over 100% of the stencil. *(See Pro Tip 3. See also Pro Tip 4, Embossed Stenciling.)* Continue the stencils everywhere and allow them to firmly dry. *(See Pro Tip 2.)*

▪▪ STEP**FIVE**

Mist a 3′ x 3′ (1m x 1m) area with water. Mix your AquaCreme with a small amount (a few drops goes a long way) of the Dark Brown AquaColor. Apply a small amount of the glaze to your "Neon Leon". In small circular motions, apply your glaze to the AquaStone. If you wish to have a more translucent glaze, either add more AquaCreme to your glaze or mist the surface with more water. *(See Pro Tip 4.)*

FINISHED TECHNIQUE

FINISHED TECHNIQUE

PROJECT TEN
CELESTIAL PLASTER

Celestial Plaster can be executed in any colors to go with your decor. The colors selected here go beautifully with the rest of this home's decorating. The reflective quality of the metallic color peaking through the multi-colored matte skip-trowel texture adds a sparkle and airiness to any room's decor. I have used this technique in kitchens, bathrooms, family rooms and foyers. Add a little sparkle to your walls and be amazed at how the reflective metallic light dances around the room.

Home of George & JoAnn Kurz

MATERIALS

2-inch (5cm) chip brush or sponge or roller

6-inch (15cm) drywall taping blade

lightweight drywall mud (topping compound)

AquaColor Dutch Metal:

  Copper

electric drill with drywall mixing blade attachment

two 5-gallon (19 liter) mixing buckets

dark coral latex paint

base color latex paint

COLOR PALETTE

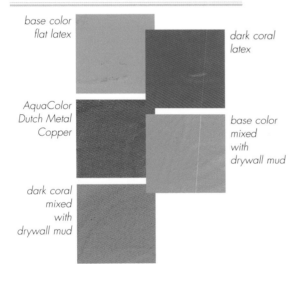

base color
flat latex

dark coral
latex

AquaColor
Dutch Metal
Copper

base color
mixed
with
drywall mud

dark coral
mixed
with
drywall mud

PREP

This technique can be used over either smooth or slightly distressed walls.

PRO TIPS

PRO TIP 1 **Using an Electric Drill to Mix**
After mixing up a large batch of this material by hand once, I quickly realized that an electric drill with a drywall mixing blade attached to it was a much better system. So now I mix the materials I will need with an electric drill and mixer in a 2- or 5-gallon (8 or 19 liters) bucket.

PRO TIP 2 **Mixing Drywall Mud with Latex Paint**
Drywall mud will change the color of the latex paint, making it lighter and chalkier in appearance. Be consistent and use the same brand of drywall mud throughout the project because each manufacturer's drywall mud is a different color.

STEP**ONE**

Apply two solid basecoats of flat latex paint computer-matched to the color in the color palette on page 59.

STEP**TWO**

You can apply this next step with a sponge, a brush or a roller. What you are looking to do is create a random pattern of large, medium and small splotches of the metallic copper paint, covering 40% of the surface area. This step (painting only part of the wall metallic) saves a lot of time and money because metallics are expensive and only about 5%–10% of the final look shows any metallics.

STEP**THREE**

(See Pro Tips 1 and 2.) Mix 2 parts lightweight drywall topping compound to 1 part of your dark coral color flat latex. Then apply this mixture over 20%–30% of the surface area with a skip-trowel technique, working in an area that is about 2' x 2' (½m x ½m) at a time. (Refer to step 2 of the Embossed Stenciling project on page 48.)

■■ STEP**FOUR**

Mix two parts of your lightweight drywall topping compound to 1 part of your flat latex base color. Apply this to your surface with a skip-trowel technique over the still wet paint from step 3.

What you're looking to do is to blend the two colors together to create a tertiary color—keeping the integrity of the first two colors and now also having the new blended color on the surface. In addition to this, you need to make sure to leave about 10% of the copper untouched so it floats and keeps its shine.

FINISHED TECHNIQUE

FINISHED TECHNIQUE

PROJECT ELEVEN
COLETTE'S CLASSIC

As an observer of life, my curiosity allows me to learn something from my students every time I teach a class. It may be how they hold their brush, their different use of color or they may share their creative ideas with me. That is the case with Colette's Classic. I was shown this finish by Colette Hayden and I fell in love with it. I had hand painted papers for years but not quite the way this is done. I like the fact that I can paint the paper at home and someone else can install it in full sheets. We have since developed a whole line of hand-painted papers for our clients. Rawhide (page 66) and Rouge Royale (page 70) are two examples.

Homearama 2003, DeStefano Homes, June Surber, Designer

MATERIALS

60 lb. brown craft paper

SofTex

rubber float trowel or 12-inch (31cm) window squeegee

Pro-FX thinner

Stain & Seal:

  Rich Brown

  American Walnut

three staining pads

LusterStone:

  Antique Parchment

craft knife

9-inch (23cm) roller with ½-inch (13mm) nap lambskin sleeve

COLOR PALETTE

Rich Brown
Stain & Seal

American
Walnut
Stain & Seal

Antique
Parchment
LusterStone

PREP

Apply this finish to a 4-foot (1m) wide, 60 lb. craft paper. You can purchase this at any paper supplier or large hardware store. It is important to do this technique on a smooth, hard surface, such as a banquet table. *(See Pro Tip 1 of the Rawhide project on page 67.)*

PRO TIPS

PRO TIP 1 Making a Notched Squeegee
To make the notched squeegee or trowel: Cut out sections carefully with a craft knife. Create a random, irregular pattern of broad areas and smaller areas.

PRO TIP 2 Using the Edge of the Table as a Guide
We use the edge of the table as a guide each time we pass the tool on the surface.

PRO TIP 3 Determining Paper Measurements
Refer to Pro Tips of the Rouge Royale project on page 71 for directions on how to measure and determine the amount of paper needed.

PRO TIP 4 To Help You Succeed
See Pro Tips 1, 2 and 3 from Rouge Royale.

PRO TIP 5 Installation
You can hang the paper yourself or have a professional wallpaper installer do the job for you. Make sure to use a quality wallpaper paste.

▪▪▪ STEP**ONE**

Working one sheet at a time, apply a medium density of SofTex over 100% of your surface with a roller.

▪▪▪ STEP**TWO**

Take your notched squeegee or trowel *(See Pro Tip 1)* and move it through the SofTex with a firm, hard pressure in as straight a line as possible. *(See Pro Tip 2.)* Complete each sheet while the SofTex is still wet. Set each sheet aside to dry fully.

▪▪▪ STEP**THREE**

Take your Rich Brown Stain & Seal and cut it 10% with Pro-FX thinner. Next, apply it with a staining pad in a vertical fashion, randomly following your striated lines and covering 50%–60% of the surface area in which you are working. You want to create varying line weights and densities with your Rich Brown stain. Be careful not to make stripes.

▪▪ STEP**FOUR**

With a different staining pad and while your Rich Brown Stain & Seal is still wet, apply the American Walnut Stain & Seal. You want to fill in the negative areas and slightly overlap the Rich Brown Stain & Seal—blending the two areas together. Complete all areas and allow to dry.

▪▪ STEP**FIVE**

With a small amount of Antique Parchment LusterStone on a different staining pad, apply it in a sparse random vertical pattern with very light pressure. Make sure to soften the transition areas between the Antique Parchment LusterStone and the two Stain & Seal colors. Allow to dry. Hang your paper in full sheets like you would any wallpaper.

FINISHED TECHNIQUE

FINISHED TECHNIQUE

PROJECT TWELVE
RAWHIDE

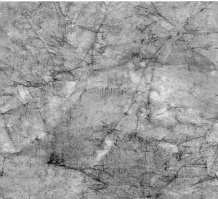

This is a hand-painted paper that is fast and easy to do. You can hang the paper yourself or have any wallpaper hanger install it. After we learned how to do Colette's Classic, we started developing our own ideas. Dave Texter, who works with me, came up with this awesome technique. This finish is suitable for any room where visible texture and a hint of metallics will work.

Homearama 2003, Hensley Homes, Henry T. Vittetoe III, Designer

MATERIALS

60 lb. brown craft paper

float trowel

stainless steel Japan scraper

Stain & Seal:

  Rich Brown

  American Walnut

LusterStone:

  Charred Gold

12-inch (31cm) window squeegee

Pro-FX thinner

9-inch (23cm) roller with ½-inch (13mm) nap lambskin sleeve

staining pad

COLOR PALETTE

Rich Brown
Stain & Seal

American
Walnut
Stain & Seal

Charred
Gold
LusterStone

PREP

Apply this finish to 4-foot (1m) wide, 60 lb. craft paper. You can purchase this at any paper supplier or large hardware store. It is important to do this technique on a smooth, hard surface, such as a banquet table. (See Pro Tip 1.)

PRO TIPS

PRO TIP 1 **Where to Paint the Paper**
We paint our papers on a 4' x 12' (1m x 4m) table which we made ourselves, but you can easily do this on a 3' x 8' (1m x 3m) banquet table. To do this, act like you're ironing a sheet and finish an area of the paper, then pull it forward to expose the rest of the unfinished paper.

PRO TIP 2 **WARNING**
Stain & Seal is very concentrated, so a little bit on your pad goes a long way.

PRO TIP 3 **Benefits of Hand-Made Paper**
One of the best ways to use this paper is in a space that has a lot of small cut-up areas as well as large open areas. The process of doing this technique on paper is quicker than doing it on a wall surface that is cut up into little areas. Also, the craft paper is an integral part of this look, since you can't crumple the wall to get the cracks in the finish.

PRO TIP 4 **Determining Paper Measurement**
Refer to Pro Tips of the Rouge Royale project on page 71 for directions on how to measure and determine the amount of paper needed.

PRO TIP 5 **Installation**
You can hang the paper yourself or have a professional wallpaper installer do the job for you. Make sure to use a quality wallpaper paste.

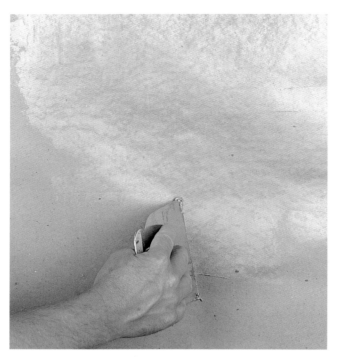

■■■ STEP**ONE**

Using your Japan scraper, apply a tight skim coat of Charred Gold LusterStone in a random pattern, covering 100% of your paper. Allow to dry.

■■ STEP**TWO**

Using your float trowel, apply a thin (1/16-inch or 2mm) random texture coat of Charred Gold LusterStone across the face of the paper. Allow to dry.

■■ STEP**THREE**

Apply the Rich Brown Stain & Seal over 100% of your surface in a thin coat using a staining pad. *(See Pro Tip 2.)*

■■ STEP**FOUR**

Crumple up the paper immediately after applying the Rich Brown Stain & Seal. Crumple loosely for larger creases which create larger cracks. Crumple tightly for smaller cracks. The cracks will form better when the paper is still slightly damp. If it dries too fast, mist the back of the paper with water before crumpling.

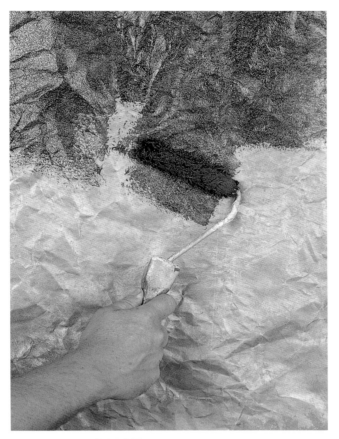

▪▪▪ STEP**FIVE**

Mix American Walnut Stain & Seal with 10% Pro-FX thinner. Roll this mixture on your paper, completely covering it with a thin layer.

▪▪▪ STEP**SIX**

While the Stain & Seal is still wet, take the window squeegee and remove all excess material from the surface, allowing the color to remain only in the cracks. *(See Pro Tip 3.)* After paper has dried completely it can be installed. *(See Pro Tip 5.)*

FINISHED TECHNIQUE

FINISHED TECHNIQUE

PROJECT THIRTEEN
ROUGE ROYALE

In the Creativity section of this book, I mentioned how we come up with new techniques and then vote on which is the best of the best. This technique tied for first place one year. I think you will agree that it is an award winner.

Home of Robert & Joni Raizk

70

MATERIALS

LusterStone:

   Mandarin Red

Stain & Seal:

   Antique Cherry

Metal Glow:

   Obsession

Royal Design Studio stencil:

   Small Flourish

   (or single overlay stencil of your choice)

"Hairy Larry" stencil brush

stainless steel trowel

40–60 lb. brown craft paper

COLOR PALETTE

Mandarin Red LusterStone

Antique Cherry Stain & Seal

Obsession Metal Glow

PREP

Load the stainless steel trowel with about a ⅜-inch (16mm) thickness of LusterStone in the color of your choice (I used Mandarin Red).

PRO TIPS

PRO TIP 1 Craft Paper Information
You will want to use either a 40- or 60-lb. craft paper. This can be purchased at any large home improvement center or at your local paper supplier. The paper comes in 3-, 4- or 5-ft. (1–2 m) widths by varying lengths per roll.

PRO TIP 2 Craft Paper Installation
The sheets of craft paper will be installed just like wallpaper. Pick a width you're comfortable installing or hire a professional wallpaper hanger to apply it for you.

PRO TIP 3 Calculating Paper Amount
To calculate the amount of paper you need: For example, for 3-ft. (1m) wide paper, figure how many strips 3-ft. (1m) wide by the height of the wall you will need to complete the room. Always make an additional strip over what you think you'll need. Deduct for windows and doors. Make sure to add 4- to 6-inches (10cm–15cm) to your total length for selvage (to trim off top and bottom) per strip. Calculate for the repeat of your pattern when determining length.

PRO TIP 4 Production-Size Stencils
You can buy production-size stencils which will increase the speed of this project tremendously.

PRO TIP 5 Using the Stencil Brush
When your stencil brush is freshly loaded, use a lighter pressure to release the material. As the brush releases material, apply a firmer pressure.

PRO TIP 6 Installation
You can hang the paper yourself or have a professional wallpaper installer do the job for you. Make sure to use a quality wallpaper paste.

▪▪ STEP**ONE**

Off-load the trowel onto the craft paper by starting your trowel at a 25° angle to the surface. Use a light pressure to release the material, dropping the angle of the blade as the material is released. Cover about 80% of your surface area with this movement.

▪▪ STEP**TWO**

Take your blade and scrape the wet material with a firm, hard pressure at a 45° angle so that it fills in all the high and low spots. Repeat steps 1 and 2 down your craft paper until it is entirely covered.

▪▪ STEP**THREE**

While the paper is still slightly damp but the paint is dry, crumple it up to create creases in your Mandarin Red LusterStone. Uncrumple the paper and allow it to fully dry.

▪▪ STEP**FOUR**

Roll on a thin coat of Antique Cherry Stain & Seal on a Whizz roller over about a 3-foot (1m) length of your paper.

■■ STEP**FIVE**

While the Stain & Seal is still wet on the surface, use a window squeegee and a firm up-and-down motion to remove the Stain & Seal in an uneven manner. Continue this process until the sheet of craft paper is completely covered. Allow to dry.

■■ STEP**SIX**

Use any stencil and color of your choice. I've used Royal Design Studio's Small Flourish stencil and Metal Glow Obsession paint color. Use your "Hairy Larry" stencil brush to apply a small, even amount of Obsession on the bottom of your brush. With a light, circular pressure, swirl the color onto your stencil, varying the pressure from light to firm. This will create an effect known as "lost and found edges." After paper has dried completely it can be installed. *(See Pro Tip 6.)*

FINISHED TECHNIQUE

PROJECT FOURTEEN
TORN PAPER

In my first book, *Great Paint Finishes for a Gorgeous Home*, I described how to do a torn paper treatment. Since then I have continued to expand on that concept. I now realize that just about any decorative finish done on a wall can also be done on paper. I always try to use the paper to its best advantage and incorporate aspects of the paper into the finish, as you have seen in the preceding projects. I just fell in love with this particular finish when it was installed in this beautiful room.

Home of Jim & Libby McFarland

MATERIALS

40 or 60 lb. craft paper

cotton rags

5-gallon (19 liter) bucket

cellulose sponge

wallpaper smoother

4-inch (10cm) Whizz roller

paint tray

9-inch (23cm) roller with ⅜-inch (16mm) nap sleeve

wallpaper size

clear heavy-duty wallpaper paste

pole extension

latex paint:

  golden brown

  eggplant

  fudge

  caramel

COLOR PALETTE

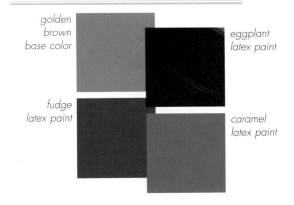

golden brown base color

eggplant latex paint

fudge latex paint

caramel latex paint

PREP

When doing our torn-paper applications, we try to work on a large, flat surface area such as a basement or garage floor. That way, we can unroll our craft paper to the length of our room and speed up our production. The total amount of paper you will need to make is roughly 60%—75% more volume than the square footage of the wall space in the room.

PRO TIPS

PRO TIP 1 Make Basecoating Easier
Speed up your basecoat by using a pole extension for your paint roller so you can paint while standing up (like mopping a floor).

PRO TIP 2 Dampen Your Rags
To keep your rags damp, fill a 5-gallon (19 liter) bucket with water. Wet your rags in the bucket and wring them back out so they are just damp. Try to keep the moisture content in your rag consistent. This will allow the paint to be removed with the same depth of color. If your rag is too damp, your paint will bead up and run on the surface. If your rag is too dry, you will not be able to get the translucent, broken-color effect you are looking for.

PRO TIP 3 WARNING
Do each consecutive step all over the paper before moving to the next step.

PRO TIP 4 Tearing Your Paper
Experiment with slicing your paper from different directions in order to achieve varied edges.

PRO TIP 5 Prepping Your Walls
If you wish to remove the paper later on, it is best to use a wallpaper size before pasting up the torn paper.

PRO TIP 6 Tips for Installing Paper Pieces
Slightly dampen the face of each piece of installed paper using water on a cellulose sponge, then use a dry rag to wipe off the face of the wet paper.

PRO TIP 7 Pasting the Paper
When pasting the paper, we have several piles of torn-up paper placed upside down on our pasting table, and we paste two or three pieces at a time. This allows us to not worry about the excess paste messing up the table because it's just getting on the next two or three pieces we're going to paste anyway.

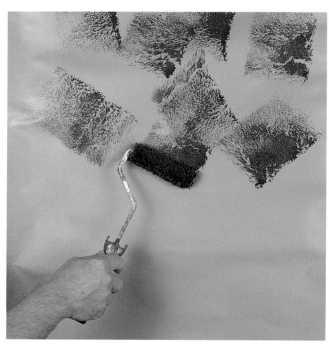

▪▪ STEP**ONE**

Once you know the amount of paper you need, basecoat all the sheets of paper at once. On a project, I will use a 9-inch (23cm) roller to apply my basecoat. One solid basecoat is usually satisfactory, though sometimes you may need to apply two basecoats, depending on the colors used. *(See Pro Tip 1.)*

▪▪ STEP**TWO**

Take your Whizz roller and apply the eggplant color in a small, random pattern. Do not work in an area larger than 1' x 2' (31cm x 61cm) because your paint will dry too quickly for you to manipulate it. This is because you are using straight latex-based paint. If you wish to open up your working time, you can mix 1 part glazing medium to 1 part latex-based paint.

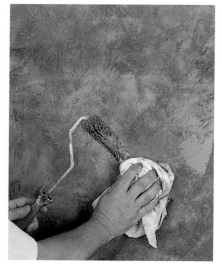

▪▪ STEP**THREE**

While your paint is still wet, use a dampened rag to pat it off. (Refer back to the Parchment, the No-Glaze Glaze and the Ralston projects for additional information. (See pages 30, 34 and 42.) *(See Pro Tips 2 and 3.)*

▪▪ STEP**FOUR**

Repeat steps 2 and 3 with the fudge color. You can use the same rag throughout this whole process. Rinse the rag between colors. I will often apply the paint using my left hand and rag off the paint using my right hand, just to help speed up the process.

▪▪ STEP**FIVE**

Again, repeat steps 2 and 3 with the caramel color.

STEP **SIX**

Once the paper is fully dry, you can then tear it into sections about the size of your hand to the size of your chest. Smaller pieces take longer to install than larger pieces, so choose wisely. For this process, my children help me a lot (and they are, by far, my most expensive laborers!). When tearing the paper, slice it back on itself to allow the edge of the craft paper to show. *(See Pro Tip 4.)*

STEP **SEVEN**

Using a heavy-duty, clear wallpaper paste, paste the back of each piece of paper and let it sit for one to two minutes before applying to the wall. You can paste four or five pieces at once. *(See Pro Tips 4 and 7.)*

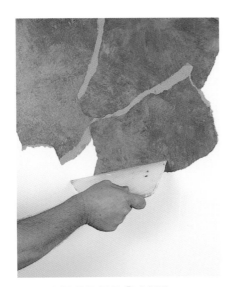

STEP **EIGHT**

Apply the paper to the wall. Overlap all pieces so no bare wall shows. Use a wallpaper smoothing tool to push excess paste out from underneath the paper to smooth it out. *(See Pro Tip 6.)* Use a sharp blade to cut excess paper off around all edges.

FINISHED TECHNIQUE

FINISHED TECHNIQUE

PROJECT FIFTEEN
HEAVEN'S GATE

I personally see the trends in decorative painting going toward textured finishes that are smoother and finishes that have metallics in them. The Heaven's Gate and Abalone treatments combine both of these together. They are both created with Venetian plasters as the main component. But unlike a Venetian plaster finish which needs to be burnished, these two do not need to be burnished to bring up the sheen. Instead other materials are used to increase the sheen level and seal the surface at the same time. I came up with the colors for this technique while one day looking at the beautiful iridescent quality of a wild turkey's feather at my local nature preserve. You never know when inspiration may strike!

Home of Judy & Roger Morris

MATERIALS

Venetian Gem:

  Brown Sapphire

Palette Deco:

  Metallic Red

  Copper

  Gold

AquaColor:

  Iridescent Green

  Iridescent Violet

  Iridescent Red

  Iridescent Orange

stainless steel Japan scraper

smoothing trowel

flat latex paint base color

medium-grit sanding block

COLOR PALETTE

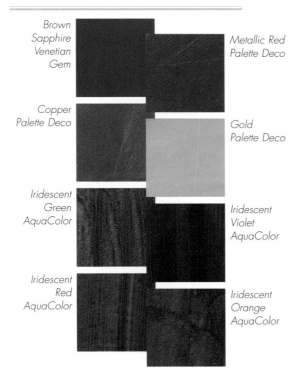

Brown Sapphire Venetian Gem

Metallic Red Palette Deco

Copper Palette Deco

Gold Palette Deco

Iridescent Green AquaColor

Iridescent Violet AquaColor

Iridescent Red AquaColor

Iridescent Orange AquaColor

PREP

Apply a basecoat of flat latex paint that is computer matched to the Brown Sapphire Venetian Gem shown on the color palette. Please read the Abalone project, pages 82–85, because it will give you information needed to do this finish as well.

PRO TIPS

PRO TIP 1 Using the Japan Scraper
All stainless steel Japan scraper blades will have a bow to the blade. You need to make sure that the bow always works away from the wall. Otherwise, the edges of the blade will create scratches in your surface.

PRO TIP 2 How to Reduce Streaking
Once you have a small area covered 100% with the AquaColor and while the surface is still wet, hold the face of the blade parallel to the wall surface and rub the surface to reduce the appearance of any streaking.

PRO TIP 3 How Much Material to Skim Coat?
For all skim coats, material will cover 400 sq. ft. (37 sq.m) per gallon (4 liters).

PRO TIP 4 How Much Material for Texture Coat?
For texture coats, material will cover 200–400 sq. ft. (19–37 sq.m) per gallon (4 liters), depending on how it is applied.

▪▪■ STEP**ONE**

Apply a tight skimcoat 100% coverage of Brown Sapphire Venetian Gem to your surface, using your stainless steel Japan scraper. Allow to dry. *(See Pro Tips 1and 2.)*

▪▪■ STEP**TWO**

Apply a texture coat of Brown Sapphire Venetian Gem using your smoothing trowel. Allow to fully dry. *(See Pro Tip 4.)*

▪▪■ STEP**THREE**

Sand the surface lightly and dust it off with a clean cloth.

▪▪■ STEP**FOUR**

Working in a small area, 2′ x 2′ (61cm x 61cm), and with a random pattern, cover the surface with 50% Metallic Red Palette Deco and 50% Metallic Copper Palette Deco. Use a stainless steel Japan scraper to apply each color. Blend them onto the surface wet-into-wet over 100% of the area. Then hold the blade at a 90° angle to the wall to scrape off all excess material. Allow to dry, which happens very quickly.

■■■ STEP**FIVE**

Apply a tight skim coat with 100% coverage with the stainless steel Japan scraper, using Metallic Gold Palette Deco.

■■■ STEP**SIX**

Using two Whizz rollers, apply the colors Iridescent Green and Iridescent Violet 50/50, wet-into-wet in a very thin, sheer application. Then scrape excess off with a Japan scraper. Allow to dry thoroughly.

■■■ STEP**SEVEN**

Use Iridescent Red and Iridescent Orange and follow the same directions as in step 6.

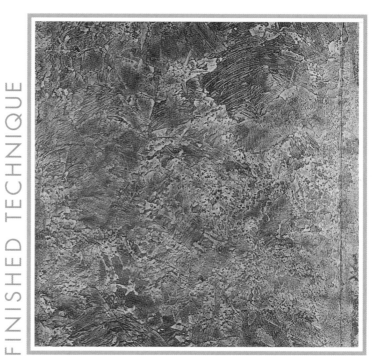

FINISHED TECHNIQUE

FINISHED TECHNIQUE

PROJECT SIXTEEN
ABALONE

The same day I created Heaven's Gate I came up with Abalone as well. I had already created a sample that took me through step 5 of this finish. But after I created Heaven's Gate and loved the addition of the iridescence on top, I decided to try that on this sample as well. I loved it and called it Crystal Blue Persuasion (another indication of my age). I later changed the name to Abalone because so many people thought that is what it looked like. This finish helped my decorative painting company win a national first place award for faux finishing.

Photo courtesy of Robin Victor Goetz

MATERIALS

Venetian Gem:

  Amethyst

  White-on-White

AquaColor:

  Iridescent Blue

  Iridescent Green

  Iridescent Violet

smoothing trowel

stainless steel Japan scraper

4-inch (10cm) Whizz rollers

flat or eggshell latex paint base color

medium-grit sanding block

COLOR PALETTE

Amethyst Venetian Gem

Amethyst and White-on-White mix

Iridescent Blue AquaColor

Iridescent Green AquaColor

Iridescent Violet AquaColor

PREP

For your basecoat, use a flat or eggshell latex paint, tinted to the color of the Amethyst Venetian Gem plaster. One basecoat is usually satisfactory. It's OK if it doesn't cover 100%. This finish works best on smooth surfaces.

PRO TIPS

PRO TIP 1 **Using the Japan Scraper**
All stainless steel Japan scraper blades will have a bow to the blade. You need to make sure that the bow always works away from the wall. Otherwise, the edges of the blade will create scratches in your surface.

PRO TIP 2 **Creating More Texture**
If, after step 5, you feel you've lost some of your texture, take a slightly damp rag, fold it flat, and with a light pressure, remove some of the last color applied. This will reveal more of your texture from below.

PRO TIP 3 **Rollers for Larger Surfaces**
When working on larger surfaces you can use a 9-inch (23cm) roller with a ⅜-inch (10mm) nap sleeve to help speed up step 6.

PRO TIP 4 **Time Saver**
If your surfaces are fairly smooth to start with, as an alternative you can use an acrylic paint, computer-matched to the Amethyst Venetian Gem, for step 1 to save labor.

PRO TIP 5 **How to Reduce Streaking**
Once you have a small area covered 100% with the AquaColor and while the surface is still wet, hold the face of the blade parallel to the wall surface and rub the surface to reduce the appearance of any streaking.

PRO TIP 6 **How Much Material to Skim Coat?**
For all skim coats, material will cover 400 sq. ft. (37 sq.m) per gallon (4 liters).

PRO TIP 7 **How Much Material for Texture Coat?**
For texture coats, material will cover 200–400 sq. ft. (19–37 sq.m) per gallon (4 liters), depending on how it is applied.

PRO TIP 8 **WARNING**
Make sure that your plaster or texture mixture is loaded on one side of the trowel only.

■■ STEP**ONE**

Apply a tight skim coat of Amethyst Venetian Gem by applying a small amount of the plaster to your stainless steel Japan scraper and off-loading it onto your surface. Then, with the blade held at a 90° angle with a firm, hard pressure, scrape excess material off until the surface is smooth. Cover all areas 100%. Allow to dry completely. *(See Pro Tips 1 and 4.)*

■■ STEP**TWO**

Using the smoothing trowel, apply a texture coat of Amethyst Venetian Gem. Place a small amount of plaster on your blade and drop the angle of the blade down so that it is almost parallel to your surface. Then, with light pressure, quickly drag the blade across the surface, and the plaster will come off in a random hit-skip pattern. The raised areas should only be ⅟₁₆-inch (2mm) or so above the surface.

If you want to flatten the areas a little more, do a compression stroke with the smoothing trowel blade. That is, place the blade flat against the surface and, with a medium pressure and quick stroke, compress the Venetian Gem plaster. Allow to dry completely.

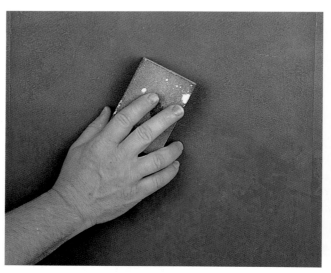

■■ STEP**THREE**

Sand the texture coat with a medium-grit sanding block, then wipe off the surface with a dry cloth to remove sanding dust.

■■ STEP**FOUR**

Mix the Amethyst Venetian Gem 50% with the White-on-White Venetian Gem. Then apply this mixture as a thin, tight skim coat over the texture coat, using the Japan scraper. Be sure to hold the blade close to the front edge so it is not flexible and is positioned at a 90° angle. Work in small areas at a time and do not overwork these areas. Two or three strokes of the mix should cover each area of your finish. Do not overlap repeatedly.

▪▪ STEP**FIVE**

Apply another tight skim coat of the pure Amethyst Venetian Gem to cover 100% of your surface. This will increase the depth of the finish. Allow to dry. It is necessary to make sure you see the texture coming through the mix at this point. *(See Pro Tip 2.)*

▪▪ STEP**SIX**

Apply a thin amount of the Iridescent Blue AquaColor, using a Whizz roller, in a small working area with 100% coverage. While this is still wet, partially remove and compress it into the surface using your stainless steel Japan scraper blade. Continue this process around the room, working wet-into-wet until your area is complete. *(See Pro Tips 3 and 5.)*

▪▪ STEP**SEVEN**

Apply equal thin amounts of Iridescent Green AquaColor onto a Whizz roller and Iridescent Violet AquaColor onto another Whizz roller. Apply them to your surface for 100% coverage, intermixing them while wet. Partially remove and compress them into the surface, using your stainless steel Japan scraper blade. Continue this process around the room, working wet-into-wet, until your area is complete.

FINISHED TECHNIQUE

FINISHED TECHNIQUE

85

PROJECT SEVENTEEN
BOOKENDS

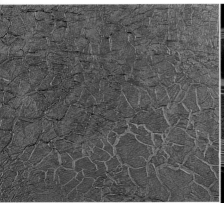

Bookends is another award-winning finish. I came up with this idea while looking at the cover of an old leather-bound book, hence the name, Bookends. I have done this finish in many studies, libraries and music rooms on walls and ceilings. If you vary the colors, you can create the look of elephant hide or reptile skin.

Home of Bryan & Kimberly Carlisle

MATERIALS

Venetian Gem:

  Ruby

AquaBond:

  Leather Red

AquaSize

CrackleMate

smoothing trowel

Palette Deco:

  Bronze

Stain and Seal:

  Van Dyke Brown

Pro-FX thinner

9-inch (23cm) Whizz roller with ½-inch (13mm) nap lambskin sleeve

cotton rags

stainless steel Japan scraper

AquaGard

COLOR PALETTE

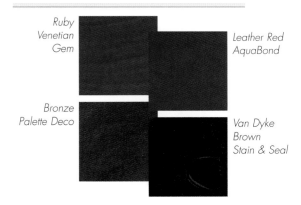

Ruby Venetian Gem

Leather Red AquaBond

Bronze Palette Deco

Van Dyke Brown Stain & Seal

PREP

For your basecoat under this finish, you can use a flat or eggshell latex paint tinted to the color of Ruby Venetian Gem. I use AquaBond Leather Red for my basecoat color. One coat of this is usually satisfactory. It's OK if this doesn't cover 100%. This technique can be done on smooth or slightly distressed walls.

PRO TIPS

PRO TIP 1 Working on Large Surfaces
When working on larger surfaces, use a 9-inch (23cm) roller with ⅛-inch (3mm) nap sleeve to speed up steps 1 and 5.

PRO TIP 2 Substituting Acrylic Paint
You can use an acrylic paint, computer-matched to Ruby Venetian Gem for your wall prep.

PRO TIP 3 Using AquaSize
AquaSize remains tacky for up to twelve hours, depending on environmental conditions. Dry heat will accelerate the dry time. Cool, damp air lengthens the dry time.

PRO TIP 4 WARNING
In step 3, you want to have material in the cracks but very little on the surface.

PRO TIP 5 Adding Pro-FX Thinner
We sometimes add up to 5% Pro-FX thinner into the Stain & Seal to make it easier to apply.

PRO TIP 6 How Much Venetian Gem is Needed?
One gallon (4 liters) of Venetian Gem will cover 100–200 sq. ft. (5–19 sq. m).

PRO TIP 7 How Much Palette Deco is Needed?
One quart (.9 liter) of Bronze Palette Deco will cover 200–400 sq. ft. (12–37 sq.m)

PRO TIP 8 How Much Stain & Seal is Need?
One quart (.9 liter) of Stain & Seal will cover 200–400 sq. ft. (19–37 sq. m).

PRO TIP 9 How Much AquaGard is Needed?
One gallon (4 liters) of AquaGard will cover 400 sq. ft. (37 sq. m).

PRO TIP 10 How Much CrackleMate is Needed?
One gallon (4 liters) of CrackleMate will cover 100–200 sq. ft. (5–19 sq. m).

PRO TIP 11 Placing Stain on the Rag
Only put a little stain on your rag (see photo.)

PRO TIP 12 Off-Loading
When working from one section into another, always off-load your tool in an area a little way from your wet edge. Work back into your wet edge—off-loading material and using increasingly lighter pressure in this transition area.

■■■ STEP**ONE**

Using the Whizz roller, apply one sheer full coat of AquaSize for 100% coverage. This material will become a translucent milky white while drying. Once the AquaSize becomes clear, you can apply a second coat of AquaSize. Two coats of AquaSize will give you larger cracks. Allow this to become clear and tacky. *(See Pro Tips 1 and 3.)*

■■■ STEP**TWO**

Mix 1 part CrackleMate with 2 parts Ruby Venetian Gem. Apply this with your smoothing trowel in a heavy (⅛-inch to ⅜-inch or 3mm to 10mm) varying thickness over the entire surface. Allow to fully dry and crack overnight. *(See Pro Tip 10.)*

■■■ STEP**THREE**

Using your Japan scraper, apply a tight skim coat of Bronze Palette Deco for 100% coverage over your entire surface. Allow to dry. *(See Pro Tips 4 and 7.)*

▪▪ STEP**FOUR**

Apply Van Dyke Brown Stain & Seal with a cotton rag using a circular motion. Feather your transition edges in and out so as not to create any lap marks. *(See Pro Tip 8.)*

▪▪ STEP**FIVE**

Apply a sheer clear coat of AquaGard Satin using a Whizz roller. Smooth out any roller marks with a soft brush while the surface is still wet, if needed. *(See Pro Tips 1 and 9.)* While the AquaGard is drying, it will be milky white but it will dry totally clear. This step will give more dimensionality and depth of color to your finish.

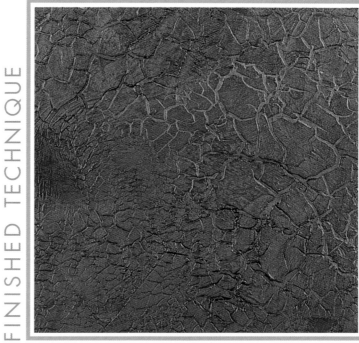

FINISHED TECHNIQUE

FINISHED TECHNIQUE

PROJECT EIGHTEEN
SHIMMER & LACE

My good friend Dave Schmidt and his wife Pam came up with this dynamic finish. I used it in this dining room and it helped us win a first place national award. You can experiment with different color foils, different lace material and different products troweled through the lace and come up with an endless variety of this beautiful finish. Try LusterStone troweled through lace; it is beautiful.

Photo courtesy of Robin Victor Goetz

MATERIALS

Rolco Slow Set Size

AquaStone

AquaCreme

AquaColor:

  Metallic Red

  Copper

  Dark Brown

  Earth Green

  Ochre Yellow

9-inch (23cm) roller with ⅝-inch (16mm) nap sleeve

6-inch (15cm) drywall taping blade

2-inch (5cm) chip brush

semi-gloss, eggshell latex, metallic paint base color

push pins

scrub brush

rags

4-inch (10cm) Whizz roller

celadon metallic foil

lace

COLOR PALETTE

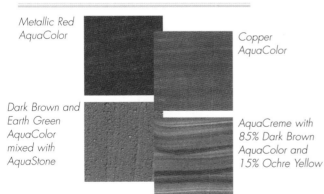

Metallic Red
AquaColor

Copper
AquaColor

Dark Brown and
Earth Green
AquaColor
mixed with
AquaStone

AquaCreme with
85% Dark Brown
AquaColor and
15% Ochre Yellow

PREP

This treatment can go over any latex-based paint. Some of the basecoat will show through in the areas where the foil doesn't transfer. Basecoat the walls in a color compatible with the foil before starting step 1. Use a semigloss, eggshell latex or a metallic paint. This technique works best over smooth or slightly distressed walls.

PRO TIPS

PRO TIP 1 Sizing
If you want to achieve fuller coverage, size an area and foil it, then re-size and foil it again. This is usually not necessary.

PRO TIP 2 Applying Foil
You can apply one piece of foil at a time or apply multiple pieces of foil, overlapping each one. It is good to do multiple pieces if your size is drying too quickly. You will not be able to see the joining seams when the finish is complete.

PRO TIP 3 Selecting Lace
For a room setting, we will buy lace curtains rather than smaller pieces of lace. What you want to look for is a large pattern. It will transfer better than a smaller pattern.

PRO TIP 4 Using the Lace for the Wall Finish
In the installation process, we bookmatch the lace seams together so that the pattern matches. Most curtain panels are wide, 54 inches (16m) or so. In step 4 you have the choice of having the whole lace panel skim coated or only sections of it. It is more time consuming and difficult to skim the whole lace panel but that is what we did on this job. If you only do selected areas, then remove the lace and just apply a texture coat of your AquaStone in the negative areas.

PRO TIP 5 When to Clean the Lace
The lace panels are good for one application and then they need to be rinsed out and dried before restarting the process.

PRO TIP 6 How Much Rolco Size is Needed?
One gallon (4 liters) of Rolco Size will cover 400 sq. ft. (37 sq. m).

PRO TIP 7 How Much AquaCreme is Needed?
One gallon (4 liters) of AquaCreme will cover 400 sq. ft. (37 sq. m).

PRO TIP 8 How Much Foil is Needed:
Measure the square footage (meters) of the area where you will apply the foil and buy 1½ times the square footage (meters).

▪▪▪ STEP**ONE**

Apply one coat 100% coverage of the Rolco Slow Set Size using the Whizz roller or a 9-inch (23cm) roller with ⅝-inch (16mm) nap sleeve. Allow the size to tack to a very sticky consistency. It should take one and one-half to three hours, depending on humidity and heat. Once it reaches its tack, it will stay tacky for an additional four to six hours. To see if you have proper tack, place your finger to the surface and release it quickly. It should make a loud popping noise if you have the correct tack. *(See foil installation on page 11.)*

▪▪▪ STEP**TWO**

Apply the metallic foil with the metallic side facing up. Using your scrub brush with a firm, even pressure, press the foil onto the tacky size. Remove the backing of the foil. The foil is not expected to transfer 100%; look for 70% and above. While the size is still tacky, you can add more foil to areas you want. *(See Pro Tips 1, 2, 6 and 8.)*

▪▪▪ STEP**THREE**

Make up a 1:1 mix of AquaColor Copper and Metallic Red. Apply this with a brush or roller to a small working area and then rag off using a hit-skip technique.

▪▪▪ STEP**FOUR**

Securely apply the lace to desired areas using push pins, so it is stretched taut. It is best to use a lace that has a large open pattern to it. I used Martha Stewart curtains from K-Mart because they were 54 inches (16m) wide and 8 feet (25m) tall. I put up four panels at a time and matched the pattern at the seams where they butted together.

Mix the AquaStone with AquaColor Dark Brown and Earth Green to your desired depth of color. Always start with a small amount of AquaColor and build up to your final color. Add 10% water and mix thoroughly. Use the drywall blade and trowel this mixture through the lace in a tight skim coat. Scrape the surface smooth using a light pressure. *(See Pro Tips 3 and 4.)*

STEP**FIVE**

Pull the lace straight up so as not to disturb your image underneath. Allow to fully dry. *(See Pro Tip 5.)*

STEP**SIX**

Mix AquaCreme with 85% AquaColor Dark Brown and 15% Ochre Yellow. Apply glaze with a 2-inch (5cm) chip brush or roller in a small working area. *(See Pro Tip 7.)* The volume of AquaCreme should exceed the amount of AquaColor used. For example, in the formula above, 1 quart (.9 liter) of AquaCreme may use 20cc of Brown and 5cc of Ochre Yellow. Always add a little color at a time to get to your desired depth of color.

STEP**SEVEN**

Soften the AquaCreme glaze while wet with a damp cloth to mottle and even out the color. You want to see the shimmer of the metallic foil through the embossed lace pattern. Continue this step around the room until all surfaces are glazed.

FINISHED TECHNIQUE

FINISHED TECHNIQUE

PROJECT NINETEEN
SAN REMI

Dave and Pam Schmidt came up with a treatment we call San Michel. We have a pattern packet for it in our *It's Faux Easy* individual technique series available on our Web site. I altered that formula in two or three areas and came up with San Remi. As an option, you can include a stencil border as an accent. This finish has been a big hit everywhere I have taught it.

Homearama 2003, DeStefano Homes, Cindy Crawford, Designer

94

MATERIALS

untinted PlasterTex

6-inch (15cm) drywall taping blade

SofTex

AquaStone

AquaCreme

AquaColor:

  Golden Sienna

  Dark Brown

  Earth Brown

  Eggplant

  Earth Green

  Van Dyke Brown

  Blue

  Ochre Yellow

terrycloth towel

three 4-inch (10cm) Whizz rollers

misting bottle

rubber trowel

sea sponge

2-inch (5cm) chip brush

COLOR PALETTE

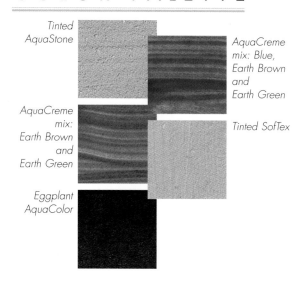

Tinted AquaStone

AquaCreme mix: Blue, Earth Brown and Earth Green

AquaCreme mix: Earth Brown and Earth Green

Tinted SofTex

Eggplant AquaColor

PREP

This treatment can be applied to any low-sheen or flat latex paint in a light to mid value. We used off-white latex. It works well over any smooth or slightly distressed wall.

PRO TIPS

PRO TIP 1 Using an Electric Drill to Mix
We find using an electric drill with a drywall mixing blade aids us when we mix our materials.

PRO TIP 2 WARNING
When rolling on the untinted PlasterTex, work in a 3' x 4' (1m x 1m) area and allow the material to dry slightly before using the trowel blade.

PRO TIP 3 Scraping Material from Walls
Scrape material off all high areas so that only the low areas get filled in—being careful not to lose the colors underneath. Scrape hard, holding the blade at a 90° angle.

PRO TIP 4 AquaStone Formula:
1 quart (.9 liter) of AquaStone *mixed with*
2 teaspoons (10ml) Golden Sienna AquaColor
1 teaspoon (5ml) Dark Brown
1 teaspoon (5ml) Earth Brown

PRO TIP 5 First Glaze Formula:
1 quart (.9 liter) AquaCreme *mixed with*
1½ tablespoons (18ml) Earth Brown

PRO TIP 6 Second Glaze Formula:
1 quart (.9 liter) AquaCreme *mixed with*
1 tablespoon (15ml) Earth Green AquaColor
⅔ tablespoon (10ml) Blue
½ tablespoon (7ml) Earth Brown

PRO TIP 7 SofTex Formula:
1 quart (.9 liter) SofTex *mixed with*
1½ tablespoons (18ml) Ochre Yellow AquaColor
1 teaspoon (5ml) Earth Brown
1 teaspoon (5ml) White
¼ teaspoon (1ml) Van Dyke Brown

PRO TIP 8 How Much PlasterTex is Needed?
One gallon (4 liters) of PlasterTex will cover 100–200 sq. ft. (5–19 sq. m).

PRO TIP 9 How Much AquaStone is Needed?
One gallon (4 liters) of AquaStone will cover 100–200 sq. ft. (5–19 sq. m).

PRO TIP 10 How Much AquaCreme is Needed?
One gallon (4 liters) of AquaCreme will cover 400 sq. ft. (37 sq. m).

PRO TIP 11 How Much SofTex is Needed?
One gallon (4 liters) of SofTex will cover 200–700 sq. ft. (19–65 sq. m).

STEP**ONE**

Thin your untinted PlasterTex with 15%
water prior to application on the wall.
Using the Whizz roller, apply a thin skim
coat of the untinted PlasterTex over 100%
of the area. Smooth with a rubber trowel
or a 6-inch (15cm) drywall taping blade.
You need to trowel this down while the
PlasterTex is not fully dry. Complete this
process around the room and allow to fully
dry. (See Pro Tip 2.)

STEP**TWO**

Using the damp sea sponge, apply the
PlasterTex in a random pattern over a small
area. Try to create a composition that has
a balance of positive and negative space
with more material in some areas and less
in others. I always look for large, medium
and small shapes. The PlasterTex should
cover about 85% of the dried skim coat at
this point. (See Pro Tip 7.)

STEP**THREE**

While the PlasterTex is still wet, lightly
knock down the high areas using the
rubber trowel. You want highs and lows in
your PlasterTex at this time. Continue this
process around the room. Allow to dry.
Once dry, use the metal trowel to scrape
the surface to bring out the sand particles
in the material.

STEP**FOUR**

Mix AquaStone with 90% Golden Sienna AquaColor, 5% Dark
Brown, 5% Earth Brown and a little water to reach desired color.
Using a 6-inch (15cm) drywall taping blade, do a random 75%
coverage in a tight skim coat of the colored AquaStone. (See Pro
Tips 1, 3, 4 and 8.)

STEP**FIVE**

Before the stone is fully dry, use the misting bottle with water to wet
your working area. Then, using a damp terrycloth towel, rag the
surface to move the AquaStone to create varying depth of color by
removing more in some areas and less in others. Allow to dry.

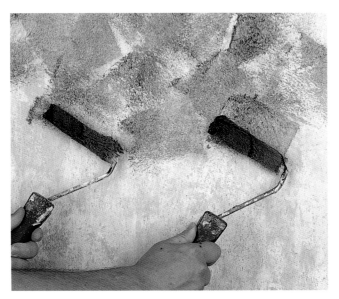

▪▪▪ STEP **SIX**

Mix up two separate glazes—the first with AquaCreme, 70% Earth Green AquaColor and 30% Earth Brown. The second glaze mixes AquaCreme with 40% Earth Green, 40% Blue and 20% Earth Brown. Mist a small working area with water and apply the two glazes with two 4-inch (10cm) Whizz rollers 50/50 in a random vertical pattern. Use your damp terrycloth towel to blend the colors together, again removing more in some areas and less in others. Allow to dry. *(See Pro Tips 5 and 9.)*

▪▪▪ STEP **SEVEN**

Mix SofTex with 70% Ochre Yellow AquaColor, 15% Earth Brown, 10% White and 5% Van Dyke Brown. Use the drywall taping blade to apply a tight skim coat to 75% of the area. You can use your wet terrycloth rag to create additional dark and light values if you wish. *(See Pro Tips 6 and 10.)*

▪▪ STEP **EIGHT**

With a 2-inch (5cm) chip brush, apply the Eggplant AquaColor in a random vertical pattern. While the AquaColor is still wet, soften the edges with a damp rag creating varying values on the surface.

FINISHED TECHNIQUE

FINISHED TECHNIQUE

PROJECT TWENTY
AGED CRUMBLED PLASTER

This is a great finish to help create an aged European flair to your room. This texture was a perfect complement to the natural wood floor, granite countertops and brick walls in this beautiful home. The finish is kept irregular on purpose to reinforce its look of natural aging. This finish will hide a multitude of sins underneath, from bad drywall to torn-up wallpaper.

Home of Brooks & Alicia Gerlinger

MATERIALS

PlasterTex

4-inch (10cm) Whizz roller

9-inch (23cm) roller with ⅜-inch nap sleeve

Lime Slag

smoothing trowel

6-inch (15cm) drywall taping blade

Stain & Seal:

   Rich Brown

Pro-FX thinner

terrycloth rags

misting bottle

2-inch (5cm) chip brush

COLOR PALETTE

Rich Brown
Stain & Seal

PREP

This finish will work over any light or mid-value latex paint in a flat or eggshell sheen. This treatment can be applied over any smooth or lightly distressed wall.

PRO TIPS

PRO TIP 1 **Selecting Your Roller**
When working on larger surfaces you can use a 9-inch (23cm) roller and ⅜-inch (10mm) nap sleeve to help speed up step 1.

PRO TIP 2 **WARNING**
Step 4 is messy so mask out accordingly.

PRO TIP 3 **Creating Translucency**
For more translucent areas, apply more Pro-FX thinner or water in step 7.

PRO TIP 4 **Using and Electric Drill for Mixing**
When mixing your products for the job site, we find it best to use an electric drill with an attached drywall mixer.

PRO TIP 5 **Selecting Your Brush**
On the job site, you can use a 4-inch (10cm) chip brush or 4-inch (10cm) Whizz roller to apply your Rich Brown Stain & Seal color.

STEP**ONE**

Using a Whizz roller, roll on a thin 100% coverage of PlasterTex that has been diluted 10%–20% with water. Lightly knock down high areas with a drywall taping blade. Allow to dry. *(See Pro Tip 1.)*

STEP**TWO**

Scrape the surface with the 6-inch (15cm) drywall taping blade to bring up the sand particles in the PlasterTex. Mix ½ teaspoon (2ml) of Lime Slag with 1 quart (.9 liter) of PlasterTex. This mix may vary. The material will be hard and crumbly and difficult to stir, so you can use an electric mixer or mix it by hand. Immediately after it becomes hard and crumbly, mix in water until the mixture becomes a thick putty-like slurry. *(See Pro Tip 4.)*

STEP**THREE**

Apply this mixture using your Whizz roller with 65% –75% coverage of the area in a random pattern, creating highs and lows of material. The higher (thicker) the material is, the more it will crack as it dries.

STEP**FOUR**

Before the material is dry, use the drywall taping blade to hit the surface with hard and firm pressure, then pull straight out and away from the surface. This will release material in some areas and spike material in others. *(See Pro Tip 2.)*

▪▪▪ STEP**FIVE**

Before the material is dry, hold the 6-inch (15cm) drywall taping blade parallel to the surface and lightly knock down the high areas. Allow to dry and crack, usually overnight.

▪▪▪ STEP**SIX**

Mist the surface lightly with water in your 2′ x 2′ (61cm x 61cm) working area. Apply Rich Brown Stain & Seal in a small, loose, random pattern.

▪▪▪ STEP**SEVEN**

While the Stain & Seal is still wet, take Pro-FX thinner or water and softly blend transitions onto your wall, with a 2-inch (5cm) chip brush. *(See Pro Tips 3 and 5.)*

▪▪▪ STEP**EIGHT**

While the surface is still wet, softly wipe out more areas with a soft terrycloth rag, creating three values of light, medium and dark on your surface. You can also do this by just pushing your stain out to a lighter value with your brush and leaving other areas darker.

FINISHED TECHNIQUE

FINISHED TECHNIQUE

PROJECT TWENTY-ONE
HOLOGRAM FOIL

This is another treatment that received a national first place award for faux finishes. This sleek contemporary finish has a rainbow iridescent quality. It is a beautiful finish that looks especially nice on ceilings and in small spaces, like bathrooms. You can also apply this foil to furniture, picture frames, columns, moldings or use it in your artwork. I did a silhouette of my city's skyline at night, and I used the hologram foil for the light in the windows and the moonlight reflected in the river below.

Photo courtesy of Robin Victor Goetz

MATERIALS

hologram foil

4-inch (10cm) Whizz roller

Rolco Slow Set Size

scrub brush

AquaCreme

AquaColor:

  Metallic Red

  Bronze

paint tray

cheesecloth

COLOR PALETTE

Metallic Red AquaColor

Bronze AquaColor

Metallic Red and Bronze mixed into AquaCreme

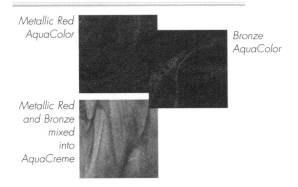

PREP

This treatment can be applied to any flat, eggshell or semi-gloss latex paint in a light or mid-value color. This treatment works best on a smooth surface.

PRO TIP

PRO TIP 1 **Choosing Color Beneath the Foil**
Because the hologram foil has many different colors, you can choose to put a soft, pastel color underneath the foil. This will then reflect back through the negative areas of the foil.

▪▪ STEP**ONE**

Apply one full coat of the Rolco Slow Set Size with the Whizz roller and allow it to tack up to a firm tack. *(Read the section on foil installation on page 11. Also see step 1, Shimmer & Lace, page 92.)*

▪▪ STEP**TWO**

You can apply the hologram foil by cutting it up into geometric shapes or tearing the edges for a ragged look. In this sample, I tore the edges, crumpled the foil, then uncrumpled it and applied it to the surface.

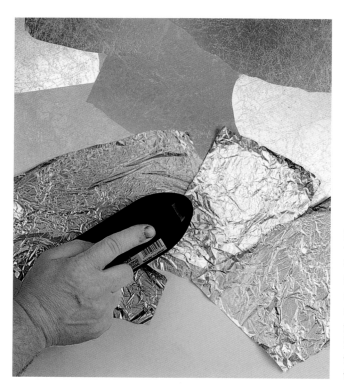

▪▪ STEP**THREE**

Make sure you apply the foil with the shiny side up. Then, with a medium to hard pressure, use your scrub brush to transfer the foil to your surface. I will usually apply five to fifteen pieces of foil, rub them to transfer the foil, remove the backing and start again.

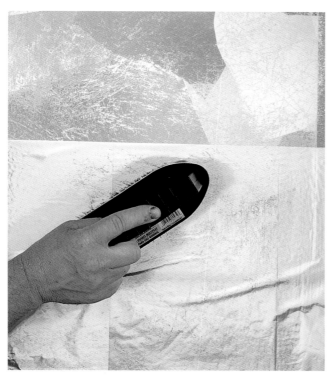

■■ ■ STEP**FOUR**

You may have to replace the foil over some areas when it does not transfer. Do not expect to cover the area 100% with the foil but look instead for 80%–95% coverage. When doing this reapplication step, you do not have to crumple the foil. The hologram will reflect light differently in the areas where it transfers now from where it was transferred before.

■■ ■ STEP**FIVE**

Tint AquaCreme with the Bronze and Metallic Red AquaColors, with equal amounts of each color. Roll the mixture on using your Whizz roller. Apply the glaze color in small 2' x 2' (61cm x 61cm) sections with 100% color. Colors can be changed to complement your decor.

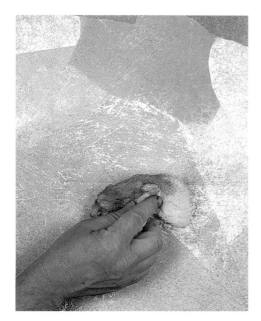

■■ ■ STEP**SIX**

While the AquaCreme is still wet, lightly pat off the surface with cheesecloth to distribute the material more evenly. Repeat steps 5 and 6 until the entire room is complete.

FINISHED TECHNIQUE

FINISHED TECHNIQUE

PROJECT TWENTY-TWO
MAN IN THE MOON

What a fun piece to make! Have the Man in the Moon shimmer at you from a ceiling or a corner of a room. You can also just do it as an art piece and frame it so you can hang it anywhere. Make the companion sun piece using the sun stencil, following the same directions, and create a set. Try another stencil with any of the foils to create an entirely different look.

MATERIALS

Dressler Stencil Company:

> *#270M Sun and Moon (or single overlay stencil of your choice)*

Palette Deco:

> *White*

AquaColor:

> *Dutch Metal Silver*

universal tints:

> *blue*
>
> *black*

misting bottle

three 2-inch (5cm) or 4-inch (10cm) chip brushes

Rolco Slow Set Size

pewter metallic foil

hologram foil

4-inch (10cm) Whizz roller

scrub brush

stencil spray adhesive

rubber trowel

cheesecloth

COLOR PALETTE

Dutch Metal Silver AquaColor

Dutch Metal Silver AquaColor, blue & black tints mixed to medium value

Dutch Metal Silver Aquacolor, blue and black tints mixed to dark value

PREP

This treatment can be applied to any flat or eggshell latex paint in a light or mid-value color. This also works best on a smooth surface.

PRO TIPS

PRO TIP 1 **Creating Dimension**
A good way to tell if your Palette Deco is high enough off the surface of the stencil is to check to see that you can barely see the stencil below.

PRO TIP 2 **Checking the Raised Material**
It is OK if the raised material is not perfectly smooth.

■■■ STEP**ONE**

As you will see, I have done this technique with both the sun and the moon stencil. You could also do this technique using a stencil of your choice. Use a stencil spray adhesive and spray the back of the stencil, then apply it flat to the surface in the area where you wish your design to be. Take your trowel blade and trowel on the White Palette Deco. The Palette Deco should cover 100% of the stencil area and should be raised off the surface of the stencil about ¼ inch (6mm). Please refer to the Embedded Stenciling and Dimensional Knockdown with Stenciling projects for further tips. Allow to dry.

■■ STEP**TWO**

Tint the Dutch Metal Silver with the blue and black universal tints to create a medium and dark value of blue-gray, with your lightest value being the Dutch Metal Silver by itself.

■■ STEP**THREE**

First mist the surface with water. Apply each color with its own brush or roller. Apply the darkest value at the top, the medium value in the middle and the straight silver at the bottom. With back and forth criss-crossing motions, blend the colors, wet-into-wet. This creates a faded transition between colors. Work two colors at a time. For example, work from dark to mid-value and then from mid-value back to dark until there is a soft transition between them. Start with the mid-value again, fade into the light area, apply the light color and blend back up into the mid-value. Work these colors wet-into-wet, back and forth, until there is a soft transition. If the paint starts to dry while blending, mist it with water again or mix with a small amount of AquaExtender. Allow to dry.

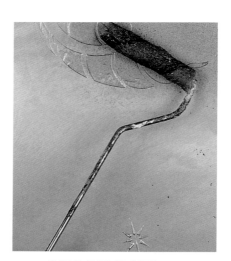

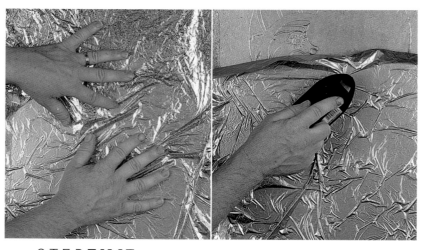

■■ STEP**FOUR**

Apply one coat of Rolco Slow Set Size and allow it to tack up to a firm tack.
(Read the section on foil installation on page 11. Also see step 1, Shimmer & Lace on page 92.)

■■ STEP**FIVE**

Crumple up the pewter foil, uncrumple it and apply it with the shiny side up. You need to make sure that you press in around your raised image for the foil to transfer. You may need to repeat this process in areas where the foil didn't transfer, as often as you like. You can use a scrub brush to help the transfer process. Apply your foil completely.

■■■ STEP **SIX**

Repeat step 3 immediately. Take a piece of cheesecloth and soften your transitions by removing some of the metallic paint color while it is still wet, revealing your foil below. Allow to dry.

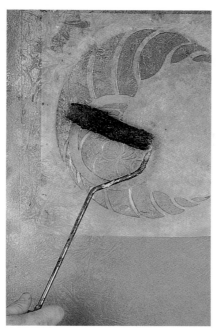

■■■ STEP **SEVEN**

Replace your stencil over the raised image. Size only that area with the Rolco Slow Set Size. Be careful to avoid any bleeding of the size from underneath the stencil. Allow it to tack up.

■■■ STEP **EIGHT**

Place the hologram foil on the raised stencil area with the shiny side up and press it firmly over the raised stencil so it will transfer.

FINISHED TECHNIQUE

PROJECT TWENTY-THREE
JEANNE'S LUSTERSTONE

If you have not used LusterStone yet, you should. It is one of the hottest products in the marketplace today. Remember earlier I mentioned I thought metallics and smoother finishes were the cutting edge of faux finishes? This product combines both in a unique, easy-to-use, beautiful product. This technique only shows you a small sample of the varied, yet breath-taking uses for this product. LusterStone comes in a wide variety of pre-made colors for your decorating needs. LusterStone is also used in the Rawhide, Rouge Royale and Penny Lane treatments in this book.

MATERIALS

4-inch (10cm) Whizz roller

9-inch (23cm) roller

LusterStone:

　Champagne Mist

　Charred Gold

smoothing trowel

stencil of your choice

stencil brush

medium-grit sandpaper

COLOR PALETTE

Champagne
Mist
LusterStone

Charred Gold
LusterStone

PREP

This technique can be applied over any light to mid-value flat or eggshell latex paint. This technique works over any smooth or slightly distressed surface.

PRO TIP

PRO TIP 1　**WARNING**

You will notice lap lines appear as you roll the LusterStone on. Do not worry. They often appear when you first start but will go away later with the additional coats.

■■■ STEP**ONE**

Apply Champagne Mist LusterStone with a 4-inch (10cm) Whizz roller or a 9-inch (23cm) roller over 100% of your surface in a thin coat. Allow to dry fully. LusterStone may be thinned up to 20% with ordinary tap water for this procedure. *(See Pro Tip 1.)*

■■■ STEP**TWO**

Apply the next coat of LusterStone with the use of a thin flexible plastic or stainless steel smoothing trowel. Put LusterStone onto the surface of the trowel. Then apply a thin coat from the trowel to the wall surface. Use smooth, even, random motions 12 inches (31cm) to 24 inches (61cm) in length. Complete this around the room. Wait at least two hours for it to dry thoroughly and then lightly sand your surface with a medium-grit sandpaper.

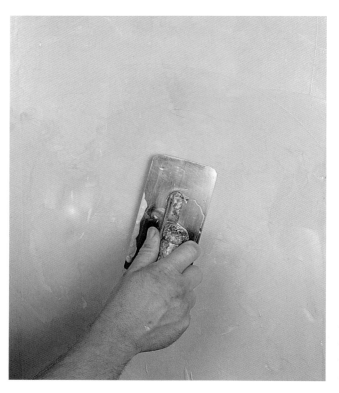

■■■ STEP**THREE**

In general, fine sanding between coats and applying very thin wet coats of LusterStone will produce the highest shine and reflectability. Sand between additional coats using fine sandpaper. LusterStone may be thinned up to 30% with ordinary tap water for this procedure. Apply very fine, very thin, wet additional coats for the highest shine. LusterStone, when applied correctly, requires no secondary polishing. No topcoat is needed for this finish. Two or three coats are enough to provide an optimum sheen. This can be a finished technique by itself. There are forty LusterStone colors to choose from. They can be intermixed to create an endless variety of colors.

▪▪▪ STEP**FOUR**

Hand cut squares of varying sizes and stencil through the squares with Charred Gold LusterStone in a random wall pattern. You could also use any stencil of your choice for this step.

▪▪▪ STEP**FIVE**

After you have all your stencils painted and dried, repeat step 3. This layering process with the stencil being wedged between the two coats can also work with any other stencils. I have done multi-layered stencils with varying shades of LusterStone for the stencil colors, for a very pretty effect.

FINISHED TECHNIQUE

FINISHED TECHNIQUE

PROJECT TWENTY-FOUR
AUTUMN LEAVES

My friends John and Greg of Pro Faux were nice enough to allow me to share one of their beautiful creations with you. Their technique is called Autumn Leaves, which is very descriptive of the actual finish. This intriguing textural finish reminds one of a beautiful Ohio day in late October. It utilizes several products, tools and techniques used in creating other textures. The final coloration can vary widely as you begin to experiment with different basecoats and top coats.

Home of Mr. & Mrs. Schuyler Smith

MATERIALS

Pro Faux Pro-Venetian Plaster:

  Red Base

Pro Faux Metallic Waxes:

  Copper

  Gold

Pro Faux Iridescent Wax:

  Russet

Pro Faux Acrylic Clear Satin Wax

Pro Faux Stonewash Pigment:

  Black

steel spatulas

natural leaves: approximately 15 leaves per sq. yd. (sq. m)

BrushStuff

cellulose sponges

medium-grit sandpaper

acrylic or oil-based flat primer sealer

red latex paint

COLOR PALETTE

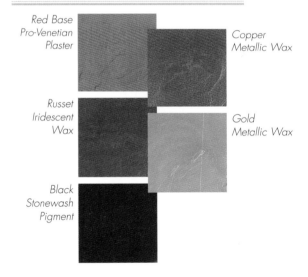

Red Base
Pro-Venetian
Plaster

Russet
Iridescent
Wax

Black
Stonewash
Pigment

Copper
Metallic Wax

Gold
Metallic Wax

PREP

Prime drywall with acrylic or oil-based flat primer sealer. Note: Pro Faux Venetian base products are actually self-priming but the sheen will flatten if used over unsealed joint compound, just like enamels. Prime surfaces that have varying porosity. Apply one basecoat of red latex over 100% of the working area. Allow to dry.

PRO TIPS

PRO TIP 1 **Sanding**
After your leaf design is dry, take a piece of medium-grit sandpaper and sand lightly to remove any raised areas.

PRO TIP 2 **Applying Glaze**
To avoid creating negatively removed areas during step 3, apply your glaze in the following fashion: In your first process, apply the Black Stonewash Pigment in a small, circular fashion in a little area. Now, for your transition areas, you will create the same process, but start away from your transition area with a firm pressure. Gradually reducing the pressure, and removing more of the glaze until you have a very light pressure and a minor amount of glaze left, work past the transition area.

PRO TIP 3 **WARNING**
The firmer your pressure and the more wax is used, the more Black Stonewash Pigment will be removed.

■■ STEP**ONE**

Using one spatula to hold a small amount of the Red Base, take a little on the second spatula and begin cross-hatching the area. Put the base on at a shallow angle (approximately 25°) and scrape off the excess nearly perpendicular to the surface. When this first application has had some time to dry (usually twenty minutes), burnish lightly to knock down any heavy texture.

■■ STEP**TWO**

Lubricate the leaves before pressing them into the wet base by diluting BrushStuff with a little warm water and wiping the leaves with a dampened sponge. Set aside. Use the spatulas once again to lay down a semi-thin bed of Red Base. Press a lubricated leaf into the wet surface, using the spatula to flatten out the leaf. Lift the leaf out and reposition it so that you can make a similar impression nearby. Rotate the position of the leaf so that the pattern does not look too repetitious. Try using the other side of the leaf as well. Repeat the process until the entire area is completed. Let texture dry several hours to overnight. Work on 1 square foot (32 sq. cm) at a time, gradually increasing the area with practice. *(See Pro Tip 1.)*

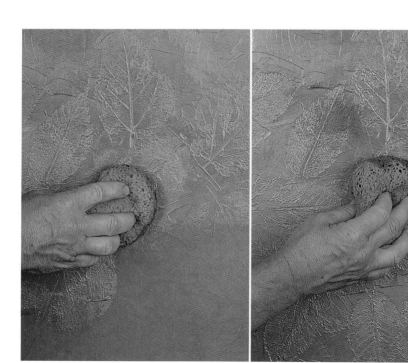

■■ STEP**THREE**

Use a dampened sponge to apply Pro Faux waxes. Apply two thin coats of Copper in small circles. Rinse sponge and highlight randomly with Russet and finally highlight with Gold. Let dry twenty to sixty minutes. *(See Pro Tip 2.)*

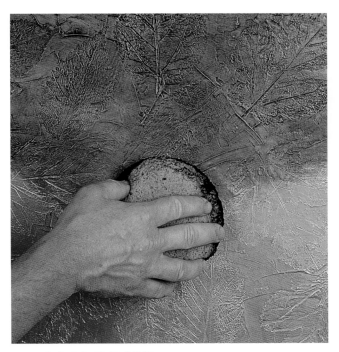

▪▪ STEP **FOUR**

Mix a small amount of Black Stonewash Pigment with water. Sponge on in circles to accentuate the leaf pattern. If it looks a little dark that's OK because the final wax will tend to lighten the overall value of the finish. *(See Pro Tip 3.)*

▪▪ STEP **FIVE**

When the Stonewash Pigment is dry, use a clean dampened sponge to apply the protective Acrylic Clear Satin Wax in small circles. Notice that if you "insist" with the rubbing, some of the Red Base peeks through! This really livens up your Autumn Leaves finish.

FINISHED TECHNIQUE

FINISHED TECHNIQUE

PROJECT TWENTY-FIVE
KITCHEN CABINET MAKEOVER

The name sounds like a reality TV show, doesn't it? In a year's time, my staff will save our clients tens of thousands of dollars by repainting their old existing cabinets. Do you want sticker shock? Get an estimate to remove your old cabinets and countertops and replace them with new custom or even stock cabinets. Ouch!!! By using this technique, you will save yourself thousands of dollars and still end up with the look of high-end custom cabinets at a fraction of the cost.

Home of Ray & Debbie Brown

MATERIALS

roller and short nap roller sleeve

cut brush

trisodium phosphate

rags

220-grit sandpaper

AquaBond: Off-white

AquaGlaze

AquaCreme

AquaGard

AquaColor: Dark Brown

2-inch (5cm) and 4-inch (10cm) chip brush

cheesecloth

caramel latex paint

HVLP sprayer (optional)

key bob (optional)

COLOR PALETTE

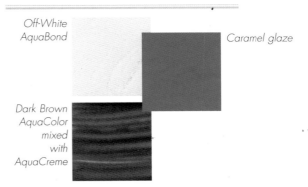

Off-White AquaBond

Caramel glaze

Dark Brown AquaColor mixed with AquaCreme

PRO TIP 1 **Using a HVLP Sprayer**

To use an HVLP (high volume/low pressure) sprayer, dilute your water-based paint between 10% and 20% so it can spray through the nozzle easily. When using spray equipment, you need to make sure that you mask out and protect your working environment from overspray. The benefit of using a spraying system vs. a brush-and-roller system is that you can apply a more even coat with fewer applications. And you end up with a more professional finish.

PRO TIP 2 **How to Make a Key Bob**

To make a key bob, get miscellaneous miscut keys (often for free) from anyone who makes keys. Then, string them onto a wire coat hanger for this purpose.

PREP 1

You need to make sure that your cabinets are clean and free of dirt, grease, wax or any other contaminant that will not allow the paint to stick to your cabinet surface. I normally use 220-grit sandpaper and do a light sand over 100% of the cabinets, always following the grain of the wood. (You do not want to sand against the grain of the wood—it looks horrible!)

PREP 2

Next, clean your cabinet with trisodium phosphate. Thoroughly rinse with water and allow to dry. You can also use lacquer thinner for cleaning but it has a much stronger odor.

■ ■ STEP**ONE**

Use a primer that will stick to the finish on your cabinetry. I like AquaBond because it can stick to almost any surface, including Formica, lacquer-based, oil-based or water-based finishes. Also, AquaBond, once dry, will sand to a very fine powder and not ball up in your sanding tool. Another excellent primer for this step is XIM.

If you're using AquaBond Off-White, as we did in this project, you can use it for your primer and basecoat combined. If you're using the XIM, you need to apply one coat of it for your primer and then use either AquaBond Off-White or a 100% acrylic eggshell paint in off-white for your basecoat.

To apply your primer and basecoat, I recommend using an HVLP sprayer. *(See Pro Tip 1.)* If this is not available, then use a short-nap roller and a cut brush, as I did.

When you use a brush and roller, always cut in the recessed areas with your brush first and then roll in as tightly as you can everywhere.

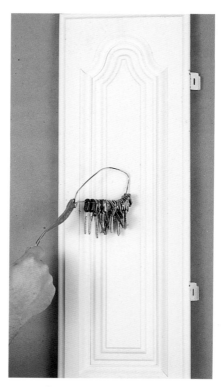

■ ■ STEP**TWO**

Before applying the final basecoat of paint, (as an option) take a key bob and distress the surface of your cabinets to your taste. *(See Pro Tip 2.)*

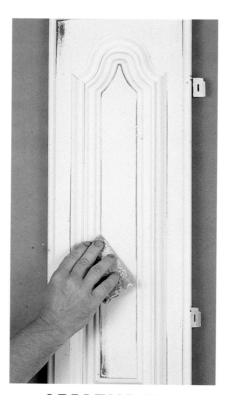

■ ■ STEP**THREE**

Another option is to sand the edges of your cabinets slightly to reveal the wood below. Always sand with the natural grain of the wood in an irregular pattern—to represent aging.

■ ■ STEP**FOUR**

Mix up a glaze with 1 part caramel latex paint and 4 parts AquaGlaze. Apply a thin amount of this using a 2-inch (5cm) or 4-inch (10cm) chip brush following the natural grain of the wood.

■ ■ STEP **SIX**

Brush Dark Brown AquaColor mixed with
AquaCreme onto the cabinet doors and wipe
off with a ball of cheesecloth, as in step 5.
AquaCreme is a clear water-based glazing
medium that you can color with any 100%
acrylic liquid paint, such as AquaColor.
AquaCreme is slow drying for easy work-
ability and dries to a very hard finish. As
an additional step, let the AquaCreme dry
and topcoat with a clean water-based sealer
like AquaGard. You can brush, roll or spray
on your final sealer coat of AquaGard.
A sprayed-on coat will give you the most
professional-looking finish.

■ ■ STEP **FIVE**

While the glaze is still wet, take a ball of
cheesecloth and remove 80% to 90% of
the glaze, following the natural grain of
the wood. Allow to dry.

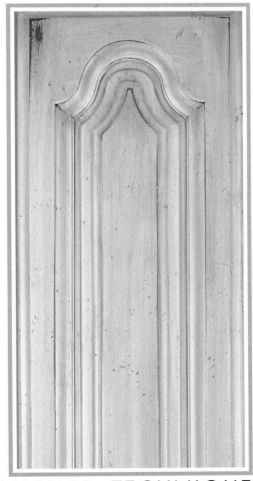

FINISHED TECHNIQUE

I am fortunate to have many talented people work with me and this finish was created by one of them. (See Creativity on page 19.) Jeff had a vision to have a blend of colors segue in and out of themselves like the colors do in a rainbow. Our palette for this job, like all projects, coordinates with other elements in the room. This technique creates an ambiance in the room that is totally distinctive and unique.

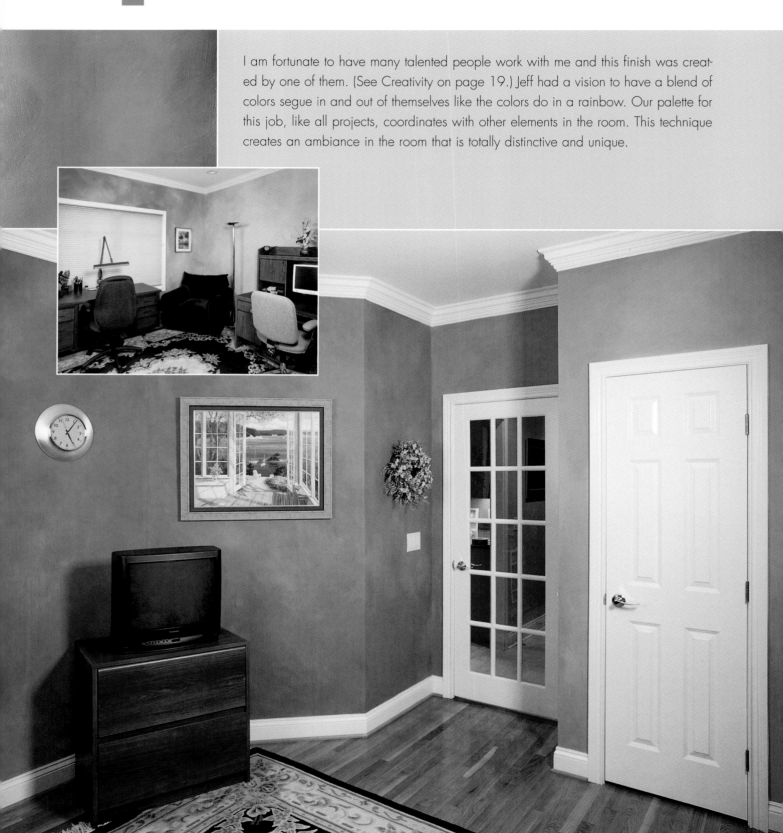

Home of Ben & Sally Chapman

MATERIALS

latex paint:

  yellow

  green

  light blue

  dark blue

multiple 2-inch (5cm) and 4-inch (10cm) chip brushes

misting bottle (optional)

glazing medium (optional)

COLOR PALETTE

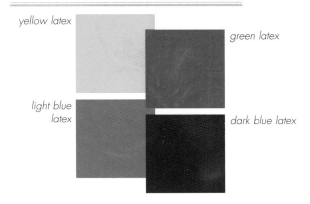

yellow latex

green latex

light blue
latex

dark blue latex

PREP

You can do this technique over any satin or eggshell latex paint in a white or off-white color.

PRO TIPS

PRO TIP 1 **Blending Colors**

To help increase your blending and allow a longer open time to work your colors, spray a light mist of water on the surface before and during blending of your colors.

PRO TIP 2 **Using Glazing Medium**

Another way to open up your working time and help your colors blend is to mix 1 part glazing medium into 1 part of each paint color.

■■■ STEP**ONE**

Using a combination of 2-inch (5cm) and 4-inch (10cm) chip brushes, apply the first color (yellow) in a cross-hatch motion— looking for 90%–100% density of the color in your working area, about 12" x 18" (31cm x 46cm).

■■■ STEP**TWO**

Using a clean brush and your green color, work slightly away from your yellow wet edge and bring the green into the yellow in a cross-hatch motion. Now, take your yellow brush and bring it from the yellow area into the green, creating a soft transition between your colors, working the colors back and forth.

■■■ STEP**THREE**

Now, take your light blue color and blend it back into your green— the way you did in step 2 with the yellow.

   When you first start your transitions, the pressure of your brush should be firm on the surface while you do a coarse transition and blending of colors. As your transitions become apparent, lighten your pressure up to create a smoother transition between the colors. To remove excess brush strokes, continue to lighten up the pressure and brush across your existing strokes at a 90° angle.

▪▪▪ STEP **FOUR**

Take the darker blue and blend into the lighter blue, as before. Continue this process around the room—using as many colors as you would like to create your rainbow. *(See Pro Tips 1 and 2.)*

FINISHED TECHNIQUE

FINISHED TECHNIQUE

PROJECT TWENTY-SEVEN
PENNY LANE

Sometimes we as artists become frustrated and disenchanted in our design making process. At times we also cannot see how pretty something is because it may not have been what we were attempting to start with. Also, there are times we just plain do not like what we came up with. Kris, a very skilled artist, came up with this finish (See Creativity on page 19) but was not pleased with it and threw it away in the garbage. I found the sample and loved it, making no changes to it at all. I have since taught this to dozens of students and sold the finish multiple times to clients. So what do we learn from this? One thing for sure, beauty is in the eye of the beholder.

Home of Frank & Lisa Veneziano

MATERIALS

drywall mud

LusterStone:

   Brown Suede

   Champagne Mist

6-inch (15cm) drywall taping blade

COLOR PALETTE

Brown Suede
  LusterStone

Champagne
Mist
LusterStone

PREP

You can apply this technique over any flat or eggshell paint in any off-white or light value. This technique is good to use over damaged walls because it hides a multitude of sins. It can also be applied over wallpaper which is well adhered to your wall. (See page 10.)

PRO TIPS

PRO TIP 1 Skip Trowel Technique

With the skip trowel technique, if you don't like an area, you can remove it by holding your blade at a 90° angle to the surface and, with a firm pressure, scraping off the material. Then reapply the material in the negative area, using the skip trowel technique.

PRO TIP 2 Applying a Tight Skim Coat

Apply a small amount of the material to your blade and then off-load it onto your surface. Hold the blade at a 90° angle with a firm, hard pressure and scrape excess material off until the surface is smooth.

■■ STEP**ONE**

Using lightweight drywall mud, apply
a skip-trowel texture to 100% of your
surface. Let dry overnight. *(Refer to
Embossed Stenciling on page 46. Also
see Pro Tip 1.)*

■■ STEP**TWO**

Using one 6-inch (15cm) drywall taping
blade, apply a tight skim coat of Brown
Suede LusterStone over your drywall mud.
You want to fill in the low areas of your
finish and scrape all the LusterStone off the
high areas. Do this 100% around your
surface and allow to dry. *(See Pro Tip 2.)*

■■ STEP**THREE**

Using your 6-inch (15cm) drywall taping blade, apply a tight skim coat with 100% coverage of Champagne Mist LusterStone. You want to have more material in the lower areas and remove some material from the higher areas. It's desirable to still see some of the Brown Suede LusterStone in both the high and low areas after this step is completed.

FINISHED TECHNIQUE

FINISHED TECHNIQUE

PROJECT TWENTY-EIGHT
MICAH KNOCKDOWN

My employee, Micah Ballard, came up with this finish that combines two different techniques into one—metallic foils and knockdown. You can find more information on foils on page 11 and more information on knockdown on page 54. What makes this finish unique is the use of a shiny metallic foil basecoat peaking through a dimensional matte-sheened texture. What this does is allow the metallic to sparkle only in the areas where light reflects off of it. This is a great finish to apply over damaged walls or wallpaper because it hides a lot of problems. (See Creativity on page 19.)

MATERIALS

Rolco Slow Set Size

silver metallic foil

"Robert Rubber" (a nylon scrub brush)

sea sponge

6-inch (15cm) drywall taping blade

roller pan

9-inch (23cm) roller with ⅜-inch (10mm) nap sleeve

AquaStone

AquaCreme

AquaColor:

  Dark Brown

cotton rags

"Leon Neon" stipple brush (optional)

COLOR PALETTE

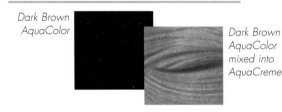

Dark Brown
AquaColor

Dark Brown
AquaColor
mixed into
AquaCreme

PREP

This treatment can go over any flat or eggshell latex paint. If you harmonize your base color with the color of your foil, you will see less background movement. If you want more movement in the background, use a lighter or contrasting color. For this technique, I used a taupe latex with an eggshell finish to harmonize with my foil.

PRO TIP

PRO TIP 1 **Glazing**

A "Leon Neon" is a perfect tool to use to help move your glaze on these types of textured finishes. Sometimes the glaze is applied so evenly that you do not need to use a cotton rag to pat off the surface. The majority of the time, I apply my glaze by dipping the "Leon Neon" brush in the glaze to just cover the very bottom of the brush. I then apply the glaze with a firm pressure and lighten up as I go into transition areas. Also see Pro Tip 2, Autumn Leaves, on page 115.

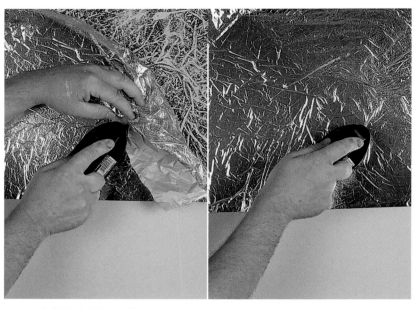

▪▪ STEP**ONE**

Apply a thin 100% coverage using the
Rolco Slow Set Size. (See information
on page 11 for applying your size and
foil. Also see step 1, Shimmer & Lace,
page 92.)

▪▪ STEP**TWO**

Crumple and uncrumple your silver metallic foil before applying it to your tacky size.
Always make sure to have the shiny side of the foil facing up. While the foil is still
adhered to the surface, use your "Robert Rubber" (nylon scrub brush) and rub firmly
over the face of the foil in a N-S-E-W direction.

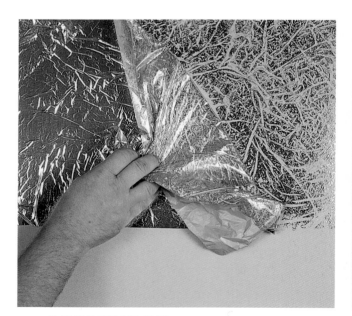

▪▪ STEP**THREE**

Remove the foil backing and continue step 2 around the room until
all areas are foiled.

▪▪ STEP**FOUR**

Taking a damp, wrung-out natural sea sponge, pat on AquaStone
which has been diluted 10% with water in a random, vertical
pattern. Look for a varying weight of the AquaStone, with small,
medium and large areas covering about 60% of your surface area.

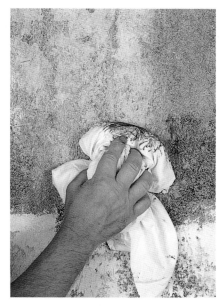

▪▪▪ STEP**FIVE**

While your AquaStone is still wet, take your 6-inch (15cm) drywall taping blade and knock down the peaks of the AquaStone. *(See Dimensional Knockdown with Stenciling on page 54.)* Final coverage should be about 70%–75% of the surface area because the AquaStone flattens out as it is knocked down. Dry fully.

▪▪▪ STEP**SIX**

Mix up Dark Brown AquaColor mixed with AquaCreme to your desired depth of color. I always test a little of the color in a small, obscure area first. Roll your Dark Brown AquaColor AquaCreme onto a 2' x 4' (½m x 1m) section and while the glaze is still wet, pat it off with a cotton rag in a firm vertical movement. *(See Pro Tip 1.)* Complete all areas with this glaze process.

▪▪▪ STEP**SEVEN**

Repeat steps 4 & 5, but deliberately aim for some of the negative areas with your AquaStone and still cover some of your original Aquastone—being careful to leave some areas untouched. Just as in step 5, knock down your AquaStone in a vertical fashion, while it is still wet, leaving only about 10% of the metallic foil untouched.

▪▪▪ STEP**EIGHT**

Repeat step 6 using the exact same glaze color and technique. If you wish your glaze to remain open a little longer, you can mist your surface with water prior to applying the glaze.

FINISHED TECHNIQUE

FINISHED TECHNIQUE

PROJECT TWENTY-NINE
DESIRÉ

This product looks so multidimensional and beautiful when completed that you will be amazed how easy and user friendly it is to do. The product is made by Adicolor (see Resource section) and comes in many different stock colors. The technique is able to work in any decor, from traditional to transitional to contemporary. Because of the subtle texture of Desiré it can also work in any room in your home, giving it a classic, durable finish.

MATERIALS

Desiré—color of your choice. I used ⅓ tinter (DT11) x ⅔ glaze

Fondo

9-inch (23cm) roller with ⅜-inch (10mm) nap sleeve

paint tray

3-inch (8cm) chip brush

plastic spatula

PREP

This treatment can go over any existing flat or eggshell latex basecoat. Pick one that harmonizes with your color of Desiré.

PRO TIPS

PRO TIP 1 Creating Paint Colors
If you cannot find a manufacturer's color that you like, select one close to what you want and alter it to the desired color by using a 100% liquid acrylic paint such as AquaColor.

PRO TIP 2 Creating an Airy or Tight Pattern
A light touch with the spatula will give the Desiré a more light and airy pattern. A firmer touch will break the particles open and create a slightly darker and tighter pattern.

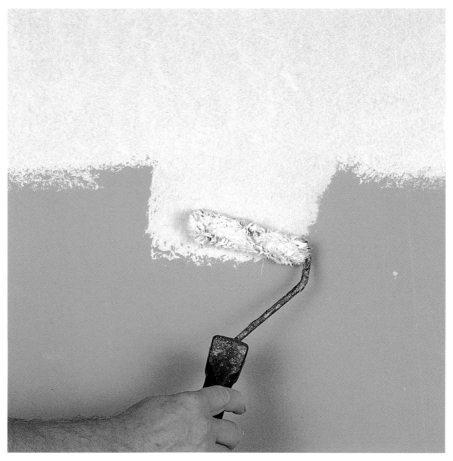

▪▪▪ STEP**ONE**

The first step is to apply a basecoat of Fondo (which is normally white) and cut it 30% with water. You can tint the Fondo to a color which harmonizes with your Desiré color if you wish. Experimentation with a variety of colors will yield many different results. We used white untinted Fondo on this project.

Apply the Fondo with a roller as you would any paint. Allow this to dry four to six hours before applying your Desiré coat. (We are applying the white Fondo onto a colored wall here. Depending on coverage, you may need to apply two coats.)

▪▪▪ STEP**TWO**

Mix the Desiré to your desired color, following the manufacturer's directions. For my sample in this book, I used color #11 ⅔ tinter with 2 liters of Desiré. The product color #11 comes in a plastic container with the measurements written on it. ⅓ tinter makes the color #11 light; ⅔ tinter makes the color #11 mid value; full tinter makes the color #11 darkest. All are mixed into a 2 liter bucket of Desiré. Pour the correct amount of tinter into your Desiré container and mix thoroughly.

Apply your mixed Desiré to your surface using a 3-inch (8cm) chip brush in a cross-hatch motion, with a light touch, like buttering toast. Work in the surface area for about ten minutes of time before you go on to the next section. Ideally, the white fluffy element of the Desiré should be randomly dispersed on the surface in a pleasing pattern of high and low areas. (See Pro Tip 1.)

■■ STEP**THREE**

Allow the material created in step 2 to remain on your surface untouched for about 5–10 minutes. Then take your plastic spatula, with a light-handed movement and with the blade held at a 45° angle to your surface, and scrape over your surface to bring up the white particles in the Desiré.

   Repeat steps 2 & 3 around your room, working from one step back to another, until your area is complete. *(See Pro Tip 2.)*

FINISHED TECHNIQUE

FINISHED TECHNIQUE

PROJECT THIRTY
CROSSED GARLAND STENCIL

Some years ago I was blessed to meet a wonderful person and very talented designer and artist, Melanie Royal. Over time we have become good friends and traveled the world together teaching decorative painting. She has a fantastic stencil company called Royal Design Studio (see the Resource section of this book). Melanie has many decorative painting books and videos that complement what I feel is one of the best stencil selections available today. This Crossed Garland stencil is from her collection. I used a combination of techniques shown earlier, to layer on top of it with lost and found edges and multicolor blended stenciling.

MATERIALS

AquaGlaze

AquaColor:

   Verdigris Dark Green

   Magenta

   Golden Sienna

latex paint:

   dark yellow

eggshell latex paint:

   butter yellow

"Hairy Larry" (large stenciling brush)

Melanie Royal Design Studio stencil:

   Crossed Garland

three 1-inch (25mm) stencil brushes

4-inch (10cm) chip brush

cotton rag

5-gallon (19 liter) bucket

COLOR PALETTE

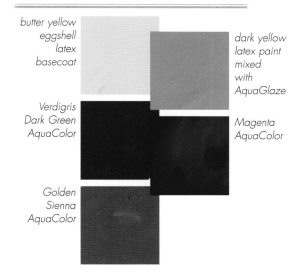

butter yellow
eggshell
latex
basecoat

dark yellow
latex paint
mixed
with
AquaGlaze

Verdigris
Dark Green
AquaColor

Magenta
AquaColor

Golden
Sienna
AquaColor

PREP

Prepare your basecoat with an eggshell latex paint in the color of your choice. I used a soft butter yellow for my base color.

PRO TIPS

PRO TIP 1 Softening Your Outside Edges
When softening out your paint with a damp rag, make sure to feather out your edges to help alleviate lap lines. (I always soften my outside edge in one area and when I bring my color back into it, I overlap my feathered areas to create the correct depth of color.)

PRO TIP 2 Using a Production Stencil
When working in a larger space, I find it beneficial to use what is termed a "production stencil." This is nothing more than six to nine of the same stencil pattern on one large sheet. By using this, it speeds up my production time tremendously.

PRO TIP 3 WARNING
Lift your stencil periodically so you can peek underneath to see if you have the saturation of color you're looking for on your surface.

■■■ STEP**ONE**

Using a 4-inch (10cm) chip brush, apply undiluted latex paint in a small area in a random fashion—covering about 30% of the wall space in the small area where you are working. Here I used a darker yellow.

■■■ STEP**TWO**

Using a damp, wrung-out cotton rag, pat out and soften your latex color—using the same hand motion described in the Two-Color Ralston project on page 34. Also read about the Parchment project on page 42. Complete this process using steps 1 and 2 around your room until all areas are finished. *(See Pro Tip 1.)*

■■■ STEP**THREE**

Make a glaze of 3 parts AquaGlaze to 1 part dark yellow latex paint. Apply this through your Crossed Garland stencil using a large stenciling brush (we affectionately call this a "Hairy Larry.") *(See Pro Tip 2.)*

On the right side you can see the resulting stencil. This is what Melanie Royal calls "lost and found" edges. Some edges are strong and apparent and others are faded out. This is created by the amount of paint on your stencil brush and the amount of pressure applied during the process. Less paint plus less pressure equals lost edges. More paint plus stronger pressure equals found edges. You can stop after this step alone and have a beautiful technique. I opted to add more color to better coordinate with the other colors in the room.

The best in **faux finishing instruction** and **inspiration** is from

NORTH LIGHT BOOKS

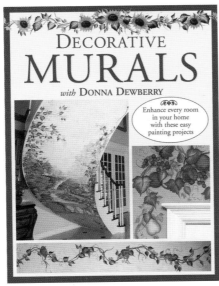

Step by step, acclaimed decorative artist Donna Dewberry shares some of her favorite tricks and techniques for creating trompe l'oeil murals, floral designs, faux finishes, popular theme designs and more. Donna's clear and encouraging instruction is filled with expert tips for doing each job a little faster and easier, along with answers to common questions about surface preparation, tools and paints! The hardest part will be deciding which gorgeous effect you want to paint first. • ISBN 0-89134-988-X, paperback, 144 pages, #31459-K

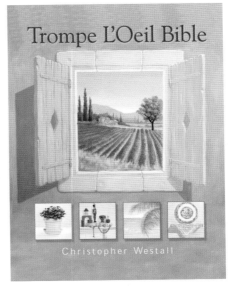

Discover a unique collection of original and inspirational trompe l'oeil motifs ideal for any home. You'll find everything you need to capture the perfect scene, from country pitcher on a shelf or climbing wisteria to curtains surrounding a window or a Greek landscape glimpsed through a marble arch. Designs include country views with a province landscape, classical views with Greek landscape, water's edge view featuring a sea-inspired landscape and more! • ISBN 0-7153-1479-3, paperback, 128 pages, #41568-K

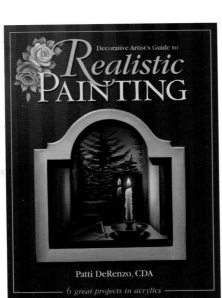

Take your decorative painting to an exciting new level of depth and dimension by creating the illusion of reality-one that transforms your work from good to extraordinary! Patti DeRenzo, CDA, shows you how to master the building blocks of realism-value, temperature, intensity and form-to render three-dimensional images with height, depth and width. • ISBN 0-89134-995-2, paperback, 128 pages, #31661-K

Learn how to create stunning illusions on walls, floors, and ceilings. Here's all the instruction you need to use inexpensive, laser-cut plastic stencils with skill and confidence. Author Melanie Royals shows you how to combine stencils, shields, and tape with simple paint techniques, buy the proper equipment, prepare surfaces, manipulate stencils, and apply paint. The final section provides more advanced instruction for large-scale projects. • ISBN 1-58180-028-2, paperback, 128 pages, #31668-K

These books and other fine **North Light** titles are available from your local art & craft retailer, bookstore, online supplier or by calling **1-800-448-0915**.

INDEX

RESOURCES

ADICOLOR, INC.
1 Applewood Crescent, Unit 2
Concord, Ontario L4K 3K1
www.adicolor.com
905-660-6686
Desiré, Fondo and other specialty products

DRESSLER STENCIL COMPANY
253 SW 41st Street
Renton, WA 98055
www.dresslerstencils.com
888-656-4515
425-656-4515
Stencils

FAUX EFFECTS
3435 Aviation Boulevard
Vero Beach, FL 32960
www.fauxfx.com
800-270-8871
*Manufacturer of Aqua Finishing Solutions
(see list of products below.)*

PRISMATIC PAINTING STUDIO
935 West Galbraith Road
Cincinnati, OH 45231
www.PrismaticPainting.com
513-931-5520
*Authorized distributor of all Aqua Finishing Solutions
products: AquaBond, AquaColors, AquaCreme,
AquaGard, AquaGlaze, AquaSize, AquaStone,
CrackleMate, Dutch Metal, Lime Slag, LusterStone,
Metal Glow, Palette Deco, PlasterTex, Pro-FX thinner,
SofTex, Stain & Seal.*

*ll brushes (badger brush, chip brush, "Leon Neon"
ippling brush, "Hairy Larry" stencil brush,
?obert Rubber" nylon scrub brush), trowels (float
wel, rubber trowel, stainless steel smoothing
wel, stainless steel Japan scraper), metallic and
gram foils, sizing (Rolco Slow Set Size) and
s (including Whizz rollers) can also be found
 website.*

*tional packets and videos are also available,
 ll as a listing of upcoming workshop classes
 nationally.*

PROFAUX
1367 Girard Street
Akron, OH 44301-2125
www.profaux.com
e-mail: John@profaux.com
330-773-1983
*Venetian plasters, waxes, stonewash pigment
and other specialty products*

ROYAL DESIGN STUDIO
2504 Transportation Avenue, Suite H
National City, CA 91950
www.royaldesignstudio.com
800-747-9767
Stencils

**THE STENCIL ARTISANS LEAGUE, INC.
(SALI)**
www.sali.org
*A non-profit educational organization committed to
promoting stenciling and the related decorative
arts through area and on-line chapters and an
annual convention.*

WORKTOOLS INTERNATIONAL
12397 Belcher Road, Suite 230
Largo, FL 33773
www.whizzrollers.com
800-767-7038
*Whizz rollers and other specialty paint tools.
These products are also available in many paint
outlets nationwide.*

■ ■ STEP **FOUR**

While your stencil is still in place and your glaze is still slightly damp, blend three colors individually over your stencil in a light swirling motion with very little color on your stencil brushes. The colors I used (in this order) were Golden Sienna, Magenta and Verdigris Dark Green. I love AquaColors as stencil paints—straight out of their containers. *(See Pro Tip 3.)*

As an option, if you wish to "age" your stencil, you can take a fine piece of sandpaper and rub it lightly—which creates a wonderful time-worn effect.

FINISHED TECHNIQUE

FINISHED TECHNIQUE